Not Algebra (math not mathing)

By: Patrice Shabazz

AF882518

Copyright © 2025 by Patrice Shabazz

All rights reserved.

No part of this publication may be reproduced, distributed, or transmitted in any form or by any means, including photocopying, recording, or other electronic or mechanical methods, without the prior written permission of the author, except in the case of brief quotations embodied in critical reviews and certain other noncommercial uses permitted by copyright law.

This is a work of [fiction/nonfiction]. Names, characters, places, and incidents are the product of the author's imagination or are used in a transformative and educational context. Any resemblance to actual persons, living or dead, or actual events is purely coincidental unless otherwise noted.

For permission requests, contact:
Patrice Shabazz
Email: patriceshabazz39@gmail.com
Publisher: Exclusive Heights

ISBN: 978-1-969629-18-1
First Edition: 2025

Cover art by Patrice Shabazz
Printed in the United States of America

This Feeling to Riches

The Mindset Shift That Breaks the Chains

Introduction: Before You Take the Leap

You're not crazy.
You're not lazy.
You're not ungrateful.

You're just doing the math.

$20,000 for dental work.
$150,000 for a home — and that's a "starter."
$35,000 for a car that depreciates the second you drive off the lot.
Food. Kids. Insurance. Debt.

And your job pays $17 an hour.
No matter how many double shifts you work… it will never add up.

That's when it hits you:
You've been lied to — gently, consistently, and with a smile.

"Work hard. Stay loyal. Be patient. And eventually… you'll be rewarded."

But you've worked hard.
You've been patient.

You've sacrificed.

And you're still in the same spot — or worse, older and more in debt.

What You're Feeling Has a Name

This book isn't about becoming rich overnight.
It's about what happens the moment you realize the system was never designed to make you free.

It's the feeling when your chest tightens after doing the math.
The cold chill when you think, "If I don't change something soon… I'll die in this."

This isn't depression.
This is awakening.

Disclaimer: What Makes the Jump Easier

This book won't promise fantasy. But if you're going to bet on yourself — stack the deck in your favor.

The leap becomes smarter when you have:

- Good Credit: Access to better rates and more financial tools
- A Vehicle: Even a used one. Movement creates opportunity
- Savings: Even $500–$1,000 can soften a fall
- Low or No Debt: You don't want new weight on top of old
- A Plan on Top of a Plan: Strategy is what separates a leap from a collapse
- Budget Down to the Last Penny: And add a 10–20% wiggle room
- A Work Ethic That Can't Be Bought: You will work harder — but this time, for you

If you have these — or if you're building toward them — this book will work for you.

What This Book Is

This is your real-time map.

Written by someone who sat in the same warehouse…

With broken cars…

Living at home…

With nothing but equipment, a dream, and the will to document everything.

This is the blueprint for going from that moment of mental rebellion —

To launching your brand, offering services, getting your first client, and building wealth by being valuable, not just used.

Let's walk it together.

CHAPTER ONE — The Programming

"The lie was beautiful. But it was still a lie."

You were born into a script.

From the first bell of kindergarten to the last clock-out at your dead-end job, you were being programmed. They didn't call it that. They called it "structure," "discipline," "stability." But it was obedience. Wrapped in tradition. Sugarcoated with phrases like:

- "Get a good job."
- "Be patient."
- "Stay out of trouble."
- "Don't rock the boat."
- "You'll get there if you just work hard."

But what if that was never true?

What if you were never supposed to "get there"? What if the only thing your loyalty built… was someone else's empire?

From the church pews to the school desks, from your mother's warnings to HR's policies — it all sounds different, but it works the same:

Sit down. Wait your turn. Be grateful for less.

By the time you realize how tight the collar is around your neck, you've already made yourself small. You're already playing not to lose. And you call it being "realistic."

But realistic to who?
To your dreams? Or to your fears?

See, the programming doesn't just happen in one place — it's layered.

School:

You're told what to memorize, not how to think. Creativity? Optional. Obedience? Mandatory. You get punished for thinking outside the box, even though the real world rewards it.

Parents (well-meaning ones):

They just wanted you to be safe. But sometimes, safety is the cage.

They were raised to believe struggle is holy — so they taught it to you like gospel.

Church:

Many Black kids are taught to wait for heaven while being crushed on Earth.

"Just keep praying. God will bless you eventually."

They don't tell you that faith without movement is poverty in costume.

HR Departments & Jobs:

Smile. Don't speak up. Ask for time off. Hope for a 25-cent raise.

And don't act like you own anything — you're just a number in a uniform.

By the time you hit 25, you're already carrying a backpack full of broken advice.

You're supposed to have the job, the car, the home, maybe a kid or two.

But instead, you're behind — and ashamed. And you blame yourself.

But how can you win if the rules were rigged?

This chapter is your wake-up call.

You didn't mess up.
You followed the script.
The problem is, the script was outdated — and designed to keep you in your place.

The Real Message of the Programming

They told you to wait your turn.
But your turn was never coming.
They told you to stay quiet.
But silence is how you disappear.
They told you to climb the ladder.
But the ladder is inside a burning building.

You were programmed to be useful — not powerful.
Polite — not dangerous.
Humble — not whole.

So what do you do?

You unlearn.

Not everything you were taught is truth.
Some of it was fear.

Some of it was survival.

Some of it was slavery passed down with new vocabulary.

Now…

You begin the process of reprogramming — not just your mind, but your actions.

You were born a creator. A builder. A solution. A spark.

You were never meant to just fit in and wait to die.

And now that you know?

You'll never sit the same again.

The Lie They Sold You

"The lie was beautiful. But it was still a lie."

From the moment you were born, you were handed a script. Not a life. Not a destiny. A script. Lines written long before you even knew your own name. A program etched into the culture, into the schools, into your family's survival habits.

That script had one command: stay in place.

The playground taught you where to stand. The bell told you when to eat. The teacher told you what to think. The church told you what to hope for. The job told you what you were worth. And every system nodded in agreement: "Don't rock the boat. Be thankful. Wait your turn."

But what if your turn was never coming?

That's the truth most never face. They think they're climbing. They think they're progressing. They think that if they just stay loyal, if they just work harder, the system will reward them. But the system was never designed to reward you. It was designed to use you.

Story One: The Boy in the Desk

There was a boy — seven years old. He loved to draw. Loved to let his imagination run. But the teacher said, "Stop doodling, pay attention." His creativity was punished. His obedience was praised.

Every time he reached for freedom, a ruler slapped his hand. Every time he questioned the assignment, a red pen slashed his paper. He wasn't dumb. He wasn't lazy. He was being programmed.

By the time he was twelve, he stopped drawing. By sixteen, he stopped asking questions. By eighteen, he had mastered the script: sit down, shut up, pass the test.

Now he's thirty-five. He's working a job he hates. And the only thing he remembers is how to follow directions.

That boy could be you. Could be me. Could be every child forced into obedience while the wealthy raise their kids to create, to own, to question everything.

Case Study: Education's Shell Game

The American education system doesn't reward the builders. It rewards the repeaters.

Over 80% of students graduate high school without ever taking a personal finance class.

College debt averages $37,000 per graduate, but the median salary for new grads is around $50k — before taxes.

Meanwhile, trade schools cost a fraction of that, but are stigmatized because the program teaches you not to own skills, but to chase status.

They tell you education is freedom. But look closer: it's debt disguised as discipline.

Who benefits? The lenders. The universities with billion-dollar endowments. The corporations who get a compliant, debt-ridden workforce desperate for a paycheck.

That's programming.

The Church Collar

For many of us, programming didn't just come from teachers. It came from the pulpit.

Every Sunday, you were told: "Be humble. Be patient. Wait on God. Suffer now, reward later."

And while you were waiting, praying, sacrificing, who was eating? The pastor with a Bentley. The church with a new sound system. The institution fattening itself while your household stayed broke.

Faith itself is not the problem. Faith is fire. Faith is vision. But faith without movement is poverty in costume. And they never taught that part.

So you learned to wait instead of work. You learned to hope instead of build. And generation after generation, Black kids were told heaven is where freedom lives — while hell was served right here on earth.

That's programming.

Story Two: The Warehouse Man

Picture this: a man in a warehouse. He clocks in at 6 a.m. He moves boxes until his back screams. He smiles when the supervisor walks by. He asks for Friday off because his child has a recital. The answer is no.

So he misses the recital. But he still smiles on Monday. He needs that check.

After ten years, the company gives him a certificate. Not ownership. Not equity. A piece of paper that says "Thanks for your loyalty."

He shows it to his son, proud but broken. The boy looks at the paper and sees the truth: his father gave ten years, and all he got was a frame.

That boy learns the script: loyalty without ownership is slavery with benefits.

That's programming.

The Military Parallel

They call it "basic training." But what is it really? Programming.

Strip you of individuality.

Replace your name with a number.

Teach you to obey without question.

Punish hesitation. Reward conformity.

Now look at the workplace. What's orientation? Basic training in a polo shirt.

Strip you of individuality: dress code.

Replace your name with a badge number.

Teach you to obey policies without question.

Punish resistance. Reward compliance.

Whether it's the drill sergeant or the HR department, the method is the same. Control the body, capture the mind, own the labor.

That's programming.

Numbers Don't Lie

Average American works 90,000 hours in a lifetime.

Median retirement savings for Black families at age 65: $24,000.

That's less than six months of living expenses.

Meanwhile, corporations post record profits every quarter.

You gave them your body. Your time. Your loyalty. And all you got was debt, stress, and maybe a pension if you're lucky.

That's not accident. That's program design.

Street vs. Corporate Programming

Now let's flip it. Look at the streets.

Young hustlers are told: "Get money. Stay loyal. Don't snitch. Don't rock the boat."

They grind day and night, but the system eats them alive — cops, courts, violence, paranoia.

Now look at corporate workers.

They're told: "Get a good job. Stay loyal. Don't complain. Don't rock the boat."

They grind day and night, but the system eats them alive — debt, stress, layoffs, sickness.

Different uniforms. Same trap.

Both are told patience will pay. Both find out patience just makes you food for someone else's table.

That's programming.

Story Three: The Silent Genius

A girl in high school aced math. She dreamed of being an engineer. But her counselor said, "That's too ambitious. Maybe nursing is safer."

So she followed the advice. Took on loans. Became a nurse. Works twelve-hour shifts.

Every night she goes home, exhausted, staring at the engineering books she never opened. She followed the script. She killed her dream.

Now she tells her daughter, “Be safe. Don’t dream too big.” And the cycle repeats.

That’s programming.

The Real Cost of Obedience

Obedience feels safe. But safety is often just control in disguise.

Obedience kept you from questioning debt.

Obedience kept you from leaving toxic jobs.

Obedience kept you from investing in yourself.

Obedience kept you waiting for permission that was never coming.

And here’s the hardest truth: the longer you obey, the harder it is to break free. The chains grow comfortable. The cage feels like home.

That’s the ultimate success of programming — when the prisoner starts defending the prison.

Case Study: The Employee Who Forgot Freedom

A study once found that workers laid off after 20+ years at one company had the hardest time adapting. Why? Because they had been programmed.

One man said: “I don’t know how to schedule myself. I only know how to follow a shift.”

Think about that. A man who lived half his life in the workplace didn’t know how to live without a time clock.

That’s not employment. That’s domestication.

The Unlearning

Programming can’t be undone with a speech. It has to be unlearned, daily.

When the system says “wait,” you move.

When the boss says “be humble,” you stand tall.

When society says “that’s not realistic,” you ask: “Realistic to who? Them or me?”

Unlearning means catching yourself when you play small. When you apologize for wanting more. When you lower your voice to make others comfortable.

Unlearning means remembering that survival isn’t holy if survival kills your spirit.

The Warning, The Story, The Lesson

The Warning:
If you don’t unlearn the programming, your children will inherit your cage and call it normal.

The Story:

A man worked thirty years at a factory. Retired with a watch and a pension check. Six months later, he died of a heart attack. His son buried him, then went back to the same factory. That's legacy under programming: debt, stress, and a cycle of wasted potential.

The Lesson:

Loyalty to a system that starves you is betrayal to your bloodline. You owe the system nothing. You owe your future everything.

Closing Manifesto

You were not born to be programmed. You were born to be free.

You were not born to wait your turn. You were born to create your turn.

You were not born to build another man's empire. You were born to build your own.

So tear up the script. Burn the program.
And remember this truth:

You were never broken. You were trained to stay small. But once you unlearn the lie, you will never sit the same again.

CHAPTER TWO — The Institutionalization

"If a man wears a uniform long enough, he forgets he was born naked."

There's a difference between being trained… and being tamed.

Most jobs don't train you — they tame you.

They don't just pay you to perform.
They pay you to forget what freedom feels like.

And after enough time… you do.

———

What Is Institutionalization?

It's what happens when you've been in a system so long,
you no longer know how to function outside of it.

Prisoners go through it.
Soldiers go through it.
Employees go through it.

It's when structure becomes your identity.
When your routines are no longer chosen — they're assigned.
When freedom starts to feel like a threat, not a gift.

Sound familiar?

How Jobs Mimic Prisons:

- Assigned Hours: You're told when to wake up, when to clock in, when to eat, and when to leave. Your time is not your own.
- Permission for Breaks: You need to ask to use the bathroom. You're an adult — asking for basic human dignity like a child.
- Surveillance: Cameras. Supervisors. Performance reviews. They say it's about safety or productivity — but it's control.
- Dress Code: Not just how you work, but how you look must conform. Your individuality is tucked under a logo.
- Punishment for Noncompliance: Show up late, get docked. Say the wrong thing, get written up. Miss a day, risk being replaced.
- No Ownership, Just Performance: You can work 10 years in the same building and own none of it. Loyalty is a one-way street.

And the saddest part?

You start believing: "This is all I can do."

The Identity Shift

When you've been on the clock too long,
you start seeing the world in shifts and schedules.
You say things like:

- "I can't take that risk right now."
- "I just need this job to hold me over."
- "I'm too tired to think about anything else."

You stop dreaming.
You stop building.
You stop remembering the feeling of making something yours.
You forget what your hands were made for.

Not just to lift boxes or answer phones.
But to create. To write. To build. To shape.

You become a ghost.
Haunting the workplace.
Clocking in and out of someone else's dream.

The Trap of Dependence

Jobs have their place — they can fund the beginning of your freedom.
But don't let the tool become the cage.

Some people are in $17/hr jobs with $70/hr destinies.
But fear makes $17 feel safe.

That's institutionalization.

It's not just physical. It's mental.
You can leave the job — and still think like an employee.
You can start a business — but still wait for permission.

You've been programmed to ask for things you already own:

- "Can I be off Friday?"
- "Can I take my vacation?"

- “Can I get a raise?”
- “Can I be seen as valuable?”

But kings don’t ask.
Builders don’t wait.
Legacy doesn’t knock — it breaks the damn door.

———

The Exit Is Mental First

Before you ever quit a job, you must quit the lie.

The lie that your value is only validated through a W-2.

The lie that your skill means nothing without a title.
The lie that ownership is only for “them.”

You are not lazy for wanting more.
You are not entitled for wanting freedom.
You are not arrogant for believing in yourself.

You’re remembering who you are.

And that remembering?

It’s the first brick in the wall you’re about to build — with your name on it.

The Uniform You Forgot You Were Wearing

“If a man wears a uniform long enough, he forgets he was born naked.”

Institutionalization isn't just something prisoners face. It's not just soldiers coming back from war who feel it. It's every worker who's been in a system so long that they no longer know how to function without it.

Think about it. The job gave you a schedule. The job gave you a paycheck. The job told you when to eat, when to rest, when to travel, when to stay put. After a while, you don't just follow it — you depend on it.

And the scariest part? You start to fear freedom.

Story One: The Man Who Asked Permission

There was a man named Dre. Worked at a warehouse 15 years. When he finally quit, his wife asked him to take a vacation. No job, no boss, no clock-in. Just him, free to go.

But when he got to the airport, something strange happened. He hesitated. He asked his wife: "Do I need to call somebody to get this time off?"

He wasn't joking. He wasn't playing. His mind had been programmed for so long that freedom felt like a violation.

That's institutionalization.

Case Study: Prison, Military, and Jobs

Prison:

Inmates ask permission to eat, sleep, and move.

Their identity is reduced to a number.

When released, many reoffend because freedom feels foreign.

Military:

Soldiers wake, train, and eat at exact times.

Every action is dictated.

When discharged, some can't function without orders. PTSD isn't just trauma — it's withdrawal from institutionalization.

Jobs:

Employees ask for vacation, bathroom breaks, and even maternity leave.

Their identity is tied to a title, badge, or position.

When laid off, many collapse because they never built value outside the uniform.

Different buildings. Same programming.

The Cage That Feels Like Home

They don't have to chain your hands if they've already chained your mind.

You believe $17/hr is better than nothing.

You believe a 25-cent raise is a blessing.

You believe being replaceable is normal.

You believe you're "lucky" just to have work.

That's the cage. It's invisible. It's quiet. But it's strong. And the worst part is, after years of living in it, you start defending it. You tell your kids, "Just get a good job, don't take risks, stay safe." You pass down the bars like they're protection, when really, they're just fear in a different form.

Story Two: The Soldier Who Couldn't Sleep

A soldier came back from Iraq. No alarms. No drills. No orders. But every morning at 5 a.m., he woke up and sat at the edge of the bed. He couldn't rest because rest felt wrong. He needed commands. Without them, he was lost.

That's institutionalization.

Now look at the worker. Fired after 20 years. He wakes up at 6 a.m. like he's still on shift. He puts on the same routine even when there's no clock to punch. Not because he loves it. But because freedom terrifies him.

That's the same sickness.

Numbers Don't Lie

70% of Americans hate their jobs, but most never leave. Why? Institutionalization.

Prison recidivism rates are 60–70%. Not because inmates want prison, but because they can't adapt to freedom.

Average job tenure is now 4 years, but employees still act like they're "lifers" because they're programmed to cling to structure.

It's not about chains. It's about comfort. And comfort can kill you just as fast as any prison cell.

The Identity Swap

When you've been institutionalized, you no longer see yourself as a person. You see yourself as a role.

"I'm a cashier."

"I'm a supervisor."

"I'm a nurse."

"I'm a soldier."

But those aren't identities. Those are positions. And positions disappear. When they do, you collapse if you don't know who you are beyond the title.

That's why people retire and die within two years. They had no identity outside the institution.

Street vs. Corporate Institutionalization

Street Hustler:

Bound by rules of the block.

Afraid to leave because loyalty is survival.

Doesn't realize the streets themselves are a prison.

Corporate Worker:

Bound by rules of the job.

Afraid to leave because the check is survival.

Doesn't realize the cubicle is just another cell.

Both think they're free because there are no visible bars. But freedom isn't the absence of bars. It's the presence of ownership.

Story Three: The Woman Who Lost Her Dream

Keisha wanted to be a writer. But she worked call centers for 20 years. Every script, every word, every break was controlled. When she finally quit, she sat at home with a notebook. But nothing came.

She realized she had been institutionalized into silence. She forgot how to think for herself.

Case Study: The Layoff Epidemic

In 2008, millions were laid off during the recession. Workers who had given decades suddenly found themselves unemployed. Many fell into depression, not just because of money, but because their entire identity was tied to the job.

One man said: "I don't know what I am without this company."

That's the danger. Institutionalization isn't just economic — it's spiritual theft.

The Trap of Dependence

Dependence makes you grateful for crumbs.

Prisoner grateful for yard time.

Soldier grateful for a day of leave.

Worker grateful for a half-day Friday.

Meanwhile, the ones who own the system are eating feasts.

You mistake dependence for loyalty. But the truth is, dependence is the leash that keeps you from running.

The Exit Is Mental First

You don't escape by quitting the job. You escape by quitting the mindset.

Stop asking for permission for what you already own.

Stop waiting for validation to use your gifts.

Stop thinking the title makes you valuable.

You were valuable the moment you were born. The system just needed you to forget.

The Warning, The Story, The Lesson

The Warning:

If you stay too long, the institution won't just control your time. It will erase your identity.

The Story:

A man retired after 30 years at the post office. First week at home, he sat in a chair all day, waiting for something to do. Second week, he withered. By the third week, he was gone. Not because his body failed, but because his spirit had nothing left to cling to.

The Lesson:

Never let a system write your identity. You are not the uniform. You are not the shift. You are not the title. You are the builder — and builders don't wait for orders.

Closing Manifesto

Institutionalization is the silent killer. It doesn't scream. It whispers. It convinces you that the cage is home, that the leash is safety, that the paycheck is freedom.

But hear this:

You were not born to live on someone else's schedule. You were not born to shrink under someone else's rules. You were not born to be institutionalized. You were born to be free.

And once you see the cage, you can't unsee it.

The question is — will you stay inside, or will you walk out and build your own?

CHAPTER THREE — The Math Ain't Mathin'

"They told you to work harder, not check the receipts."

There's a moment in every person's life where they do the math…
And finally realize the numbers were never meant to add up.

Not for you.

Not in this system.

———

Let's Break It Down:

- Teeth fixed the right way? $20,000+
- A decent home? $150,000 minimum — and that's if you find land, beat zoning, get insurance, and don't get scammed.
- Kids and a family? $35,000–$50,000 per year — daycare, food, clothes, school, time.
- Marriage or long-term commitment? $15,000–$40,000 in the first year alone if done right.
- Car? $30,000 with interest — just for something decent and reliable.
- Healthcare, phone bill, groceries, inflation, insurance, taxes, gas, savings, debt, self-care…

Now stack that against the average income.

$17/hour.
Full time? That's around $30,000–$36,000/year before taxes.

With no equity. No ownership. No passive income. No freedom.

So here's the truth:

You're not broke because you're lazy.
You're broke because the system is overpriced… and rigged.

———

The Lie of "If You Just Work Harder…"

You can't out-hustle a rigged game.
You can't fix inflation with overtime.
You can't work enough hours to buy back your life.

And that's the part they don't want you to realize.

Because once you do the math — real math —
You start questioning the whole thing.

You start asking:

- Why is school debt $80K for a job that pays $40K?
- Why do apartments cost more than mortgages?
- Why does a broken tooth bankrupt people in the richest nation on earth?
- Why am I expected to grind like a millionaire just to survive like a peasant?

———

The System is Designed to Keep You "Grateful"

Grateful for scraps.

Grateful for paychecks that vanish the moment they clear.

Grateful for "benefits" that barely benefit you.

Grateful for jobs that overwork and underpay — because "at least you have one."

But gratitude without truth becomes slavery.

And the truth is…

You are underpaid.
You are undervalued.
You are under attack — by design.

And every time you think about escaping, someone says:

"You better be thankful. You got it better than most."

No. You just see the trap clearer than most.

Now That You Know…

Now that you've done the math and seen the margins,
What will you do?

Will you go numb?

Keep showing up to a game where the house always wins?

Or will you bet on the one asset they can't duplicate?

You.

You've already seen behind the curtain.
You've already figured out the math.

Now it's time to flip the formula.

When the Numbers Betray You

"They told you to work harder, not check the receipts."

At some point, everybody has that moment. You're staring at your bills. You're staring at your paycheck. And the math just don't math. You run the numbers again, thinking you must have made a mistake. But it wasn't you.

It was them.

The system was designed to look like it adds up — as long as you don't look too close. That's why they keep you tired. That's why they keep you entertained. Because the second you slow down and calculate the truth, the illusion cracks.

And once you see it, you can't unsee it.

Story One: The Grocery Aisle Collapse

There's a brother in the grocery store. Paycheck just hit Friday, rent gone by Monday. He's pushing a cart, sweating in his hoodie, calculator open on his phone. Every beep at the register feels like a punch in the gut. Milk, bread, meat, detergent — $120.

He looks at his wallet. He looks at his kid. And that's when it hits him: "Damn… the math don't add up. I'm not broke because I'm lazy. I'm broke because the game is rigged."

That realization is heavier than any debt. It's the moment you stop blaming yourself and start blaming the system.

Case Study: Wages vs. Costs

Let's run it clean.

Median U.S. wage: \$17–\$20/hr → \$34k–\$40k a year.

Average apartment rent: \$1,200–\$1,800/month = \$15k–\$22k a year.

Childcare per kid: \$10k–\$15k a year.

Food costs for a family: \$8k–\$12k a year.

Healthcare premiums: \$6k–\$10k a year.

Transportation (car loan, gas, insurance): \$7k–\$9k a year.

That's \$46k–\$68k in costs against a \$34k salary. You're already underwater before you even touch debt, savings, clothes, or emergencies.

The math don't add up because it was never designed to.

The Student Loan Trap

They said: “Go to school, it’ll pay off.” But here’s the breakdown:

Average student loan debt: $37,000.

Average entry-level salary for Black graduates: $28,000–$35,000.

Monthly loan payment: $300–$400.

So you’re already spending 15% of your check before you even touch rent or food. Meanwhile, the universities post billion-dollar endowments, banks eat interest for decades, and you’re called “lazy” for struggling.

That’s not education. That’s extortion in a cap and gown.

Story Two: The Tooth That Cost a Fortune

A sister cracks a molar eating popcorn. Goes to the dentist. The fix? $4,000 for a crown. Insurance covers $800. She’s stuck with $3,200.

She makes $17/hr. That’s 188 hours of work — almost five weeks of full-time labor — just to cover one tooth.

That ain’t healthcare. That’s highway robbery with a smile.

Now multiply that by braces, root canals, surgery, or a child’s emergency. That’s why medical debt is the number one cause of bankruptcy in America.

The math don’t math.

Street Math vs. Corporate Math

Street Hustler Math:

Buy an ounce → flip for double.

Pay the plug, pay the crew, stash the rest.

Risk? Jail, violence, paranoia.

Endgame? Most never scale beyond survival.

Corporate Math:

Hire you for $17/hr.

You generate $200/hr in value for the company.

They pocket $183/hr.

Risk? None — for them. All — for you.

Endgame? You stay broke while they scale into billions.

Both hustlers and corporations operate on margins. The difference? Corporations are legal hustlers, backed by government, banks, and tax codes. And you? You're the product.

That's the math they don't teach.

Case Study: The 2008 Collapse

When the housing market crashed, millions lost homes. Why? Because the math was rigged. Adjustable-rate mortgages ballooned from $800 to $2,000 a month overnight.

Banks got bailed out with billions. Workers got evicted. Families got split. Depression skyrocketed.

And yet, the same banks that destroyed neighborhoods are still profiting today.

If that ain't proof the math don't math, I don't know what is.

The Lie of "Work Harder"

They say: "Just pick up more shifts." But more shifts don't stop inflation. More hours don't stop rent hikes.

If your check goes up 10% but inflation goes up 20%, you're running backwards.

Working harder is like bailing water from a sinking ship with a coffee cup. You sweat, you hustle, you grind — and the hole gets bigger.

That's why people work 60 hours and still can't pay rent. The issue ain't effort. It's the equation.

Story Three: The Uber Hustle

Marcus lost his job during the pandemic. Picked up Uber full-time. Drove 60 hours a week. Brought in $1,200. Gas took $300. Car note $400. Insurance $150. Maintenance $100.

Left with $250. Divide that by 60 hours: $4 an hour.

Marcus ain't lazy. He ain't stupid. He's a prisoner of math that don't add up.

Gratitude vs. Trap

They program you to be grateful.

Grateful for jobs that don't pay rent.

Grateful for benefits that don't benefit.

Grateful for raises that can't keep up with groceries.

Gratitude without truth is slavery. They want you to smile at crumbs while they eat the feast.

But once you see the margins, once you run the real math, you realize gratitude alone won't free you.

Numbers Don't Lie (Again)

Median Black household wealth: $24,000.

Median White household wealth: $188,000.

Cost of raising a child: $233,000 before age 18.

Average retirement savings for most Americans: Less than $65,000.

So when they say: "Just save more, just work harder," what they really mean is: "Stay quiet while the math buries you."

Case Study: Payday Loan Parasites

Over 12 million Americans use payday loans each year. Average loan: $375. Average fees: $520.

That means people pay $895 just to borrow $375.

It's not bad money management. It's engineered theft. Designed to trap the poor in a cycle that feeds billion-dollar lenders.

The math don't math — because it was never math. It was manipulation.

The Awakening

The power isn't in escaping debt. The power is in seeing it. Once you realize the system ain't broken but perfectly designed to keep you broke, you stop playing.

You stop asking for permission. You stop waiting for a raise. You stop thinking loyalty will save you.

You start betting on yourself. Because betting on them already proved fatal.

The Warning, The Story, The Lesson

The Warning:
If you ignore the math, you'll die working and still owe. The system will bury you in debt and call it "the American Dream."

The Story:
A man worked 40 years. Saved $100k. Inflation ate half. Medical bills ate the rest. He died with nothing left but

bills for his kids. His entire life was labor, but the math erased it.

The Lesson:

Don't fight harder inside a rigged system. Flip the system. Change the equation. The only math that matters is ownership, freedom, and legacy.

Closing Manifesto

The math ain't broken. It ain't flawed. It ain't failing. It's doing exactly what it was designed to do — keep you tired, grateful, and broke while the few eat everything.

But once you see it, you're dangerous. Because now you know:

You can't outwork a rigged game. But you can outthink it. You can outbuild it. You can flip the formula.

The numbers don't lie. But neither does your hunger. And when you stop playing their game and start writing your own, you finally get the only math that matters:

Riches in freedom. Riches in time. Riches in purpose.

And that equation? That's yours.

CHAPTER FOUR — The Flip Begins

"The first rebellion happens in the mind."

Before you ever quit a job, build a business, or chase a dream —

There's a moment.

A quiet, dangerous moment.

You sit at a red light or lay in your bed staring at the ceiling,

and the voice inside says:

"What if I'm not crazy?"

"What if I'm not lazy?"

"What if I was never supposed to live like this?"

That's the flip.
Not the money. Not the move.
The mindset.

The Lie You Start Unlearning

All your life, you've been taught:

- "Be grateful for any job."
- "Be loyal and patient — your time will come."
- "If you want more, you're being greedy."

But now… you're noticing things.

You see the managers with broken marriages and broken backs.

You see the elders with 40 years of labor and nothing to show for it but pills and regret.

You see people getting laid off who gave their lives to these companies.

You see time moving — fast.

And you realize: you're next.

That's when something inside you flips.

Not into anger.
Into clarity.

You Start Asking Forbidden Questions

- "What if school didn't prepare me — it programmed me?"
- "What if jobs aren't supposed to free me — just manage me?"
- "What if my life's worth isn't in a resume — but in a vision I've been too afraid to commit to?"

These thoughts are dangerous — not because they're wrong —
but because they're true.

And if they're true…
You can't go back to "normal" anymore.

You're different now.

You've seen the math.
You've seen the system.

You've seen what happens when you wait your turn — and the line never moves.

But What If I Fail?

You will.

Something will go wrong.
Someone will doubt you.
You'll waste money. You'll second-guess yourself. You'll get tired.

But here's the truth:

You're already failing if you stay.
Not because you're not surviving.
But because surviving without purpose slowly kills your soul.

So the question isn't:

"What if it doesn't work?"
The real question is:
"What if it does?"

What if one move changes your bloodline?
What if one leap gives you the wings you didn't know you had?

The Flip Begins…

The flip begins when you stop waiting for permission.

It begins when your "what if" becomes "why not."

It begins when your excuses get drowned out by your vision.

So here's your warning:

Once you flip, the system will try to flip you back.

It will tempt you with comfort, distract you with fear, and guilt you with comparisons.

But don't fall for it.

Because once your mind has tasted freedom —
Nothing else feels like home.

CHAPTER FIVE — Making the First Move

"The first door never opens until you knock."

There's a strange fear that creeps in when you try to do something different.

It's not the fear of failing.
It's the fear of starting.

Picking up the phone.
Walking into that business.
Saying, "Hey, I offer something. Can I show you?"

To most people, that sounds small.
But to someone used to hiding behind jobs, titles, uniforms, or silence —
That's a war.

———

Why It Feels Like Life or Death

Because in your mind, this first move isn't just about business.
It's about identity.

If they say "no," it feels like they're rejecting you.
Your worth. Your belief. Your leap.

But the truth is:
Most people aren't rejecting you — they're just not ready for what you offer.
And that's okay. Because you're not for everybody.

But you are for somebody.

And the only way you find that "somebody" is by moving.

The Hardest Step Is the One With No Applause

Nobody claps when you walk into that barbershop.
Nobody cheers when you cold call 15 businesses.
Nobody throws you a party when you film your first shaky video or hand out your first flyer.

But that silence?
That's where legends are born.

Because legends don't wait for validation — they move without it.

They know:

- One "yes" can change everything.
- One connection can unlock your whole network.
- One reel. One conversation. One pitch can be the start of your freedom.

So they move — even if their hands shake while doing it.

How to Reframe the Fear

Don't think of it as selling.
Think of it as sharing.

You're not bothering people — you're offering value.

You're not desperate — you're determined.

You're not begging — you're betting on yourself.

Rejection isn't a death sentence.

It's just redirection.

The more you hear "no," the closer you get to a room full of "yes."

———

Here's What to Tell Yourself Before You Knock:

- "They need me more than I need them — they just don't know it yet."
- "I'm not asking for charity — I'm showing up with solutions."
- "This is my moment. And I won't let fear rob me twice."

Then walk in.

Not arrogant.

But anchored.

Anchored in your purpose.

Anchored in your plan.

Anchored in the truth that you're doing something most people never do:

Choosing yourself.

———

So what's the first move?

Make the call.
Walk in.
Ask the question.
Film the pitch.
Hit publish.

You don't have to be perfect.
You just have to be present.

"The first door never opens until you knock."

Everybody wants the breakthrough. Everybody wants the moment. But most never even make it to the first move. They're waiting for a sign. Waiting for perfect timing. Waiting for permission.

But the truth is this: there is no perfect timing. The first move will always feel clumsy, scary, too early, too small. The first move is never comfortable — and that's why it's holy.

You don't become free because the system lets you go. You become free the moment you knock on a door without waiting for applause.

Story One: The Barbershop Pitch

There was a young brother named Malik. He had a camera. He had a vision. But he had no clients. Every night, he scrolled Instagram looking at “influencers” with polished reels, thinking, “I could do that… if only somebody gave me a chance.”

One day, he walked into the neighborhood barbershop. Hands sweating, voice trembling, he said: “Yo, I film. Let me shoot a promo for y’all, on me. Just let me show you.”

The barbers laughed. Some ignored him. But one chair said yes. Malik shot the video. Edited it in his bedroom on a cracked laptop. Posted it online. That one video got 3,000 views.

By the next month, three more shops called. By the end of the year, Malik wasn’t begging for chances — he was turning them down.

The difference wasn’t skill. It was movement.

The Psychology of Starting

The reason the first move feels impossible is because we confuse rejection with death. You walk into a business, you pitch yourself, and if they say no, your mind screams: “You’re worthless. Go back home.”

But the truth is simpler: they're not saying no to you. They're saying no to themselves, to their timing, to their budget, to their imagination.

Your job isn't to be accepted. Your job is to knock. And knock again. And again. Until the door cracks open — because the one thing no gatekeeper can ignore forever is consistency.

Case Study: Corporate First Moves

Steve Jobs: First move wasn't Apple. It was calling up Hewlett-Packard as a teenager, asking for spare parts. Boldness built the blueprint.

Oprah Winfrey: First move wasn't fame. It was pushing herself onto radio at 17, a space that didn't want her.

Nipsey Hussle: First move wasn't a record deal. It was selling CDs out the trunk until the labels came to him.

They all share one trait: they moved before applause.

Story Two: The Cold Calls

Tasha hated her job. But she loved baking. She decided to sell cakes. She made a list of 20 local businesses — cafés, barber shops, nail salons. She picked up the phone.

Fifteen hung up. Three said no. Two said, "Bring one by."

Those two became her first clients. Those clients told others. Within a year, she quit her job.

The lesson? The no's don't matter. The yeses feed you.

Street vs. Corporate First Moves

Street First Move:

Young hustler hits the corner. First sale is shaky. Heart pounding. He fumbles the bag. But once he does it once, he's in the game.

Corporate First Move:

Young entrepreneur cold-emails a company. No response. Sends another. Then another. On the tenth try, somebody replies. He's in the game.

Both require courage. Both require rejection tolerance. Both are wars against fear. The difference? One ends in prison. The other ends in ownership.

Why Silence Kills Dreams

Most people don't fail because they tried. They fail because they never knocked.

They let fear freeze them. They let comfort seduce them. They let excuses disguise themselves as strategy.

"I'll start when I have more money."

"I'll start when I learn more."

"I'll start when I feel ready."

But readiness never comes. Silence becomes permanent. And the graveyards are full of first moves never made.

Numbers Don't Lie

Average millionaire has 7 income streams. None of them started perfect.

90% of small businesses fail, but most of those were people who never adjusted after the first move. The survivors weren't smarter — they were stubborn.

It takes 7–12 contacts before a sale. That means rejection isn't failure. It's math. Every no is a step toward the yes.

Story Three: The Musician on the Corner

Jamal played guitar on the corner. For months, people walked by. Sometimes they dropped a dollar. Sometimes they didn't. One night, a club owner passed by. Stopped. Listened. Asked Jamal to play inside. That gig led to another, then another.

Years later, Jamal toured the world. People said: "You're lucky that club owner walked by." But luck didn't put Jamal on the corner. Movement did.

Case Study: Fear of Rejection in Numbers

Psychologists ran a study: one group of people was told to ask strangers for small favors every day for 30 days

— borrowing a pen, asking for directions, requesting a slice of pizza.

At first, rejection crushed them. But by week three, rejection stopped hurting. By week four, they realized rejection had no power at all.

That's the secret: fear shrinks with exposure. The first move isn't about the result. It's about building the muscle.

The First Move in the Digital Age

Today, the first move might not be a handshake. It might be hitting publish.

The first video you post with shaky audio.

The first blog with typos.

The first beat that nobody listens to.

The first skit that gets 12 views.

The silence is brutal. But silence is the test. If you can keep moving without applause, you're already ahead of 90% of people who quit after one try.

Story Four: The Silent Launch

Keon launched a clothing brand. First drop: 25 hoodies. Sold 3. He was embarrassed. Thought about quitting. But instead, he wore the hoodies himself. Kept posting. Kept showing up.

By his fourth drop, he sold out. By his sixth, he had a storefront. The first move looked like failure. But it was foundation.

The Street Law: Movement Attracts Respect

On the block, people don't respect the loud talker. They respect the mover. The one who shows up rain or shine. The one who takes the risk.

The same is true in business. Clients, investors, mentors — they don't respect words. They respect movement. They respect proof.

The first move is your proof.

The Warning, The Story, The Lesson

The Warning:

If you never make the first move, the door will never open. And the longer you wait, the heavier fear becomes.

The Story:

A man dreamed of writing a book. He talked about it for 30 years. Told his kids, his wife, his friends. But he never wrote the first page. He died with nothing but a story that never left his mind. His children never saw his gift. His legacy was silence.

The Lesson:

The world doesn't owe you a moment. You owe the world your movement. Don't wait for permission. Don't wait for applause. Don't wait for timing. Move.

Closing Manifesto

The first move is ugly. The first move is shaky. The first move is lonely. But the first move is sacred.

Because it's the moment you stop being a prisoner of fear and start being a builder of freedom.

Nobody claps at the first knock. But the sound of your fist on that door is the sound of chains breaking.

Move. Even if your voice shakes. Even if your hands tremble. Move. Because the first move is the proof that you're alive.

CHAPTER SIX — Becoming the Product

"Nobody takes you seriously… until you do."

You thought the hard part was building the skill.

Learning the craft. Writing the books. Buying the camera. Practicing the pitch.

But in this game?

You are the product.

People don't buy your service.

They buy your image.

They buy your presence.

They buy your belief in yourself.

And if you show up looking unsure, smelling like stress, moving like chaos —

That's what they feel.

That's what they judge.

———

Why You Gotta Look Like Purpose

You walk into a business with your dreads done, turtleneck crisp, coat tailored, camera bag tight, skin glowing, breath clean, scent bold, posture confident —

You don't even have to speak yet.

You already said enough.

You don't need luxury.

You need clarity.

Intentional. Sharp. Strategic.

A man who looks like he knows what he's doing can enter any room.

Because most people are looking for certainty — and you wear it.

———

Smelling Like Value

Don't underestimate smell.

When you walk past, people should remember something warm, bold, unforgettable.

That's branding.

That's impact.

Smelling good is spiritual.

It's psychological.

It's a signal that you care — and when you care about you, others will too.

Pair that scent with eye contact and a firm voice?

You just became a walking brand.

———

Moving Like Royalty

Royalty isn't about being rich.

It's about being rooted.

- Speak slower.
- Stand straighter.
- Move with calm precision.
- Don't overexplain. Don't oversell. Just be.

When you move like you already belong, people don't question your presence — they respect it.

———

But What If I'm Still Struggling?

That's the beautiful part:
You dress for the life you're building, not the one you're stuck in.

You can be broke — but sharp.
Living with your mom — but clean.
Still healing — but presentable.

People don't see your bank account.
They see your discipline.

That's what inspires trust.
That's what makes a client say,
"Yeah, I'll work with him."

———

You Are the Commercial

Everywhere you go — you're marketing.
How you speak.
How you dress.
What you carry.
What you smell like.
What you give off.

Even when you're not talking — you're talking.

So be intentional.

Become the billboard.
Become the proof.
Become the brand.

———

You are the product.

Package yourself like you cost something.
Because you do.

You Are the Brand Before the Business

"They won't buy the product until they buy you."

Everybody thinks the hustle starts with the item — the clothes, the camera, the food, the service. But the truth is harsher: people don't buy the thing. They buy the person behind it.

Your skill might get you in the room, but your presence decides if you stay. Your product might be good, but your image, reputation, and consistency decide if you eat.

The hustle doesn't start when you sell. The hustle starts when you realize: you are the product.

Story One: The Man in the Suit

Darryl was broke. But he needed clients. He couldn't afford luxury clothes, but he hit the thrift shop. Found a sharp gray suit for $12. Paid another $20 for tailoring.

The first time he walked into a meeting wearing that suit, everything changed. The receptionist smiled different. The manager shook his hand firmer. The conversation went smoother.

Did the suit give him new skills? No. But the suit packaged him differently. And in a world that judges before it listens, packaging is everything.

That $32 suit made him $3,200 that month.

That's the power of becoming the product.

The Psychology of Image

Humans are wired to judge in seconds. Before you speak, before you prove, before you pitch, you're already being measured.

The hustler with dirty shoes loses trust before he opens his mouth.

The worker with sloppy posture gets skipped for promotion.

The entrepreneur with bad energy gets ghosted after one meeting.

Fair? Maybe not. Real? Absolutely.

And once you understand that, you stop complaining about perception — and you start weaponizing it.

Case Study: Corporate Branding vs. Street Branding

Corporate Branding:

Apple sells the feeling of "different."

Nike sells "greatness" more than shoes.

Starbucks sells "comfort" more than coffee.

Street Branding:

A hustler's sneakers, car, and chains signal credibility.

The block respects the look before the numbers.

A man who moves sloppy never earns trust.

Both worlds run on the same principle: presentation is power. If you don't control your image, somebody else will define it for you.

Story Two: The Silent Close

Tasha was selling candles. She went to a local event. Her table looked plain — cheap cloth, no signs, no vibe. People walked by.

Next month, she reinvested $100. Branded bags. A clean table runner. Scent samples. She dressed sharp and smiled like she owned the room.

Same candles. Different packaging. She sold out.

The product didn't change. She did.

Becoming the Walking Billboard

The richest people don't just sell — they embody.

Nipsey wore his brand.

Jay-Z turned his name into an empire.

Even Warren Buffet became "the frugal billionaire" — an image that sells his authenticity.

You are the walking billboard. Every conversation, every post, every handshake is advertising. The question is: what are you advertising?

Numbers Don't Lie

People form opinions within 7 seconds of meeting you.

82% of investors say they invest in the person, not the idea.

Black consumers spend $1.6 trillion annually, most of it on brands they trust.

So if corporations are profiting off trust and image, why wouldn't you?

Street vs. Corporate Parallels

The Street Hustler:

Must package product clean, weigh it right, deliver consistently. If the product is trash, word spreads fast.

The Corporate Hustler:

Must package service sharp, price it right, deliver consistently. If the product is trash, reviews spread fast.

Both worlds live and die by reputation. Both worlds prove the same truth: the product is only as strong as the person behind it.

Story Three: The Broke but Sharp Closer

Chris had no money. But he studied posture, tone, and confidence. He walked into businesses like he belonged. He spoke with authority.

Half the time, his product wasn't even the best. But his presence sold it. People said: "I don't even know why, but I trust you."

That trust made him money before the product ever did.

The Trap of Hiding Behind the Product

Too many people hide. They think: "If I just make something great, it will sell itself."

Lie.

There are thousands of great products that die in silence because the creator never became the face. If people don't know you, they won't know what you make.

And if people don't trust you, they won't trust your product.

Case Study: Nipsey Hussle's Marathon

Nipsey didn't just sell music. He sold ownership, authenticity, and community. That's why he could charge $100 for a mixtape and sell out.

People weren't just buying tracks. They were buying him — his story, his stance, his brand.

That's the blueprint.

Story Four: The Corporate Pitch

Monique pitched her cleaning business to a corporate office. First time, she came in with cheap flyers and nervous energy. They brushed her off.

She came back six months later. Branded polo. Professional proposal. Clear confidence. Same service. Different packaging. She landed the contract.

That one shift fed her family for years.

The Science of Trust

Trust isn't built by logic. It's built by presentation.

Your clothes tell people if you're disciplined.

Your tone tells people if you're confident.

Your consistency tells people if you're reliable.

Before they buy, they run the unspoken math: "Do I trust this person?"

Becoming the product means controlling that math.

Numbers Don't Lie (Again)

70% of small businesses fail because of poor marketing and branding. Not bad products — bad packaging.

60% of buyers say brand reputation is more important than price.

First impressions impact long-term trust more than later actions.

Translation: your product starts with you.

The Warning, The Story, The Lesson

The Warning:

If you don't become the product, your work will stay invisible. Someone with half your talent but double your presence will eat before you do.

The Story:

A brother created apps for years. Brilliant code. Amazing design. But nobody knew him. Meanwhile, a less-talented developer built a personal brand online, posted daily, spoke confidently. He landed contracts. The coder stayed broke.

The Lesson:

Don't just build in silence. Build in presence. Your skill may be the seed, but your image is the soil. Without both, nothing grows.

Closing Manifesto

You've been told to "stay humble." You've been told to "let the work speak." But in a world this loud, silence is suicide.

Becoming the product doesn't mean arrogance. It means ownership. It means packaging your truth so the world has no choice but to see it.

The game was never about the product. The game was always about you. Once they buy you, they'll buy everything you touch.

So sharpen your presence. Guard your reputation. Become the brand. Because you don't just sell — you are the sale.

CHAPTER SEVEN — Building Without Permission

"Nobody's coming to hand you the mic. You have to speak anyway."

There will be no golden gate opening.
No boss tapping your shoulder saying, "You're ready."
No certification that suddenly makes your voice matter.

The truth?
Most people who changed the world… weren't qualified when they started.
They just refused to wait for permission.

———

The Myth of Credentials

They told you:
- "Get a degree first."
- "Work your way up."
- "You need experience."

But here's what they didn't say:
- Many who "made it" faked it until they could back it up.
- Most companies don't care what you know — just how confident you seem.
- Credentials are often gatekeeping tools to filter out the bold.

That's not to say education has no value.

But don't confuse validation with value.

You don't need a license to speak truth.
You don't need a résumé to offer vision.
You don't need permission to build impact.

———

Document. Sell. Solve. Show Up.

This is your 4-step blueprint.

1. Document
Film the journey. Record your thoughts. Capture the process.
Show people how you built what you're building — even if it's messy.

2. Sell
You don't need a business loan to offer a service.
You don't need a storefront to sell a product.
If you solve a problem — people will pay.

3. Solve
Be useful.
Not loud. Not viral. Useful.
If you make someone's day easier, their brand cleaner, their life better — you'll never go hungry.

4. Show Up
Physically. Emotionally. Digitally.
Be where you say you'll be. Keep showing your face. Keep knocking on the door.
Eventually, it opens.

———

Resume Can't Match Presence

You can hand someone a printed list of your skills.

Or you can walk in the room and show them why they need you.

You can beg for an interview.

Or you can let your consistency speak louder than a cover letter.

In today's world, people trust presence over paperwork.

They trust energy.

They trust delivery.

If you show up with integrity, style, and skill — you win.

Even without the "right" background.

———

Proof Over Praise

Don't wait to be liked.

Be undeniable.

Post your work.

Talk your vision.

Write your ideas.

Share your value.

They'll call it "bragging."

You call it building.

———

You were never meant to wait for an open door.

Kick the wall down.
Set up your own table.
And start feeding people.

CHAPTER EIGHT — "If I Quit, I Can Fly"

"The ground is familiar. But the sky is yours."

You've been staring at the exit for months.

Knowing damn well this job was never meant to carry your destiny.

But something keeps you there.

Security? Fear? Guilt?

The paycheck is small — but it's predictable.

The work is draining — but it's familiar.

The ceiling is low — but at least it's a ceiling.

And yet, there's this feeling in your chest every day:

"If I don't leave now, I might never become who I'm meant to be."

———

Fear Is a Tool, Not a Truth

Fear isn't always a liar — but it's not your god either.

Fear says:

- "What if I fail?"
- "What if no one supports me?"
- "What if I lose everything?"

But here's the real question:

"What if I don't try — and nothing ever changes?"

Fear can't make decisions for you anymore.

It's part of the conversation, not the conclusion.

The goal is not to eliminate fear.
The goal is to move with it.

———

Quitting Without Strategy Is Suicide

Let's be clear:
Quitting a job doesn't make you a boss.
Quitting with a plan does.

Before you walk:

- Build a product or skill.
- Secure 2–5 clients.
- Stack 3 months of expenses if possible.
- Have a system, not just a story.

This ain't about proving a point.
It's about protecting your leap.

The best flights come from planned takeoffs, not emotional jumps.

———

Flip the Risk

You think quitting is risky?
Let's flip that.

Risk is:

- Staying at a job where your raise is $0.50 a year.
- Letting your soul rot while you wait for Friday.

- Knowing the math doesn't work… and doing it anyway.

Risk is betting your entire life on someone else's approval.

Starting your own path isn't risky.
It's responsible.

At least when you fail on your own terms, you learn.
You adjust.
You own it.

What Happens When You Finally Jump?

Your heart pounds.
Your palms sweat.
And your eyes widen…

Because for the first time in years, the world is open again.

You start noticing opportunity everywhere.
Your instincts return.
You sharpen up.
You tap into your hunger.

That's what freedom does.

It doesn't coddle you.
It sharpens you.

And suddenly you realize:

You were never lazy.
You were just locked in the wrong cage.

———

You don't quit because it's easy.
You quit because your legacy demands it.

And when you jump with vision, strategy, and belief

—

you don't fall.

You fly.

The Edge Between Fear and Freedom

"They told you quitting was failure. But sometimes quitting is the only way to live."

We're programmed to believe quitting is weakness. That if you just hold on long enough, if you grind harder, if you sacrifice more, somehow the system will reward you. But the truth is darker: the system doesn't reward loyalty. It punishes it.

Every day you stay in a job that starves your soul, you're not being loyal — you're being buried.

There comes a point where staying is more dangerous than leaving. And when that point arrives, quitting isn't cowardice. Quitting is flight.

Story One: The Warehouse Walkout

Tyrone worked nights at the warehouse. Twelve hours. Steel-toe boots cutting into his heels. Supervisor barking. Paycheck barely covering bills.

One night, he looked around and realized every man in that building was broken. Bad backs, lost dreams, bitter hearts. He thought: "If I stay here, this building will kill me before my time."

So on his lunch break, he left his badge on the table and walked out. No speech. No goodbye. Just freedom in silence.

The next morning, he woke up scared. Rent was due. But for the first time in years, he felt air in his lungs. He didn't know what came next — but he knew staying would've been death.

That's quitting as resurrection.

The Myth of Security

They sell you "job security." But the truth is:

One layoff can erase your "security."

One injury can end your "career."

One manager's mood can end your "future."

Security in a system you don't own is slavery in costume. The real security isn't in staying. It's in owning your moves.

Case Study: Strategic Quitters

Jeff Bezos: Left Wall Street to start Amazon. People called him crazy. Now he controls empires.

Issa Rae: Quit college track. Picked up a camera. Built Insecure.

Nipsey Hussle: Quit chasing labels. Built his own grind. Died a legend, not a slave.

They all share one thing: they quit before the world clapped.

Story Two: The Nurse Who Collapsed

Keisha was a nurse. Twelve-hour shifts. Double shifts. Always on call. She thought loyalty would pay off. One day, during her shift, she fainted. Doctors told her she was burned out, malnourished, exhausted.

She cried in the hospital bed, realizing the truth: she gave her life to a system that would replace her tomorrow.

She quit. Started her own health coaching business. Struggled at first, but eventually built freedom.

Her body almost died, but her spirit finally lived.

The Risk Equation

Yes, quitting is risk. But staying is risk too. The question is: which risk feeds you?

Risk of quitting: struggle, rejection, uncertainty.

Risk of staying: sickness, regret, spiritual death.

One risk hurts now but heals later. The other feels safe now but kills you slowly.

The system only tells you about one risk. I'm here to tell you about the other.

Street vs. Corporate Quitting

Street Quitting:

Hustler leaves the game before prison swallows him. Takes skills to business. Survives.

Others refuse to quit. End up caged or dead.

Corporate Quitting:

Worker leaves the job before layoffs or burnout. Builds their own lane. Survives.

Others refuse to quit. End up broke or bitter after 30 years of "loyalty."

Both worlds prove the same law: quit early enough, or the system will quit you permanently.

Story Three: The Two Brothers

Marcus and Jamal worked at the same plant. Marcus quit at 29. Started landscaping. At first, people laughed. By 40, he owned five trucks, ten workers, steady contracts.

Jamal stayed. By 40, he had back problems, layoffs, and resentment.

Same bloodline. Same start. Different endings. The difference was one word: quit.

Numbers Don't Lie

Median job tenure: 4 years. Yet people act like their company is family.

Over 40% of workers report burnout.

70% of Americans hate their job.

Average millionaire failed or "quit" at least 3 ventures before success.

The math shows quitting isn't failure. Quitting is part of the formula.

The Emotional Wall

The hardest part of quitting isn't money. It's shame.

Your family says: "Why would you leave a good job?"

Your friends say: "I wish I had what you have."

Your mind says: "What if I fall?"

But shame is just fear disguised as advice. Most people projecting it never had the courage to move themselves. Don't take directions from the stuck.

Case Study: Emotional vs. Strategic Quits

Emotional Quit: Storms out. No plan. Ends up struggling, bitter, sometimes crawling back.

Strategic Quit: Saves up, builds skills, lines up side hustles. Leaves when the math works.

The first is escape. The second is flight. And flight is the difference between falling and flying.

Story Four: The Teacher Who Prepared

Mr. Johnson taught high school. Hated it. But he planned his exit. Saved for two years. Built a tutoring side hustle.

When he quit, his wife panicked. But within a year, his tutoring business made double his teaching salary.

That wasn't luck. That was strategy.

Numbers Don't Lie (Again)

55% of new businesses fail in 5 years. But the other 45% succeed — and most succeed because the founder quit the wrong lane to enter the right one.

Side hustles now make up $50 billion a year in income. Most start as people "quitting" nights and weekends at jobs to invest in themselves.

Quitting ain't death. Quitting is redirection.

Why the World Fears Quitters

The system hates quitters because quitters can't be controlled.

A prisoner who escapes can't be monetized.

A soldier who deserts can't be deployed.

A worker who walks out can't be exploited.

That's why they call quitting "failure." Because they fear what happens when you finally realize the door was always unlocked.

The Warning, The Story, The Lesson

The Warning:

If you stay too long, quitting won't be a choice. It'll be forced — through layoffs, sickness, or death.

The Story:

A man worked 35 years at the plant. Planned to retire at 65. At 64, the plant shut down. He got nothing but a pink slip. He cried in the parking lot, realizing he gave his life to a system that never loved him.

The Lesson:

Quit before they quit you. Flight is not weakness. Flight is wisdom. Don't wait for collapse to free yourself. Freedom requires a leap.

Closing Manifesto

They told you quitting is weakness. But the truth is, staying in cages is weakness.

Quitting isn't death. Quitting is wings. Quitting is refusal. Quitting is resurrection.

If I quit, I can fly. If I stay, I will die. And I'd rather die trying to fly than live forever in a cage.

So take the leap. Burn the badge. Close the uniform. Walk out of the system that starves you.

Because the moment you quit their plan, you begin writing your own.

CHAPTER NINE — From This Feeling to Riches

"You felt the trap. Then you built the key."

Some people chase riches without feeling the pain first.

They chase cars, condos, and clout…
But they never really had to face themselves.

You did.

You looked around and realized:

"This can't be life — not for me."

That moment? That raw, breaking-point moment?
That's the real beginning of wealth.

Because you weren't just chasing paper.
You were chasing power.
Control. Freedom. A life that's yours.

———

The Riches You Were Really After

Forget the dollar amount.
Let's talk about what you really wanted:

- Rich in time – so you could breathe again.
- Rich in freedom – so no boss owns your hours.
- Rich in presence – so your kids don't get your leftovers.

- Rich in confidence – so no room makes you shrink.
- Rich in purpose – so you wake up with direction.

That's what this journey was always about.
Not just more money.
More meaning.

———

The Journey Is Ugly. But Damn… the View.

Let's be real:

- You'll cry some nights.
- You'll second-guess yourself.
- You'll be broke in moments.
- You'll feel overlooked, underestimated, and alone.

But every time you push through?
You build a version of yourself that can never be owned again.

And when the money starts coming in…
When people start recognizing your name…
When your old job tries to rehire you…
You won't even be bitter.

You'll smile.

Because you didn't just win.

You grew.

———

What Comes Next?

You keep building.
You stack offers.
You scale your systems.
You hire your team.
You reinvest in your name.
You start leading the very people who thought they had no way out.

You don't go back.
You bring others forward.

Your riches are your blueprint.
Your story is someone else's permission.

And it all started with that one feeling…

"This job will never be enough."

That feeling was the match.
You?
You lit the fire.

Freedom Ain't Free — It's Scheduled

"Everybody wants freedom. Few want the discipline that buys it."

We talk about success like it's a blessing that falls from the sky. But blessings without discipline turn into burdens. Money without discipline becomes debt. Time without discipline becomes waste. Freedom without discipline becomes chaos.

Discipline is the gatekeeper. It's the price you pay to not fall back into slavery. And the system knows it — that's why it trains you for obedience, not discipline. Because obedience makes you useful to them. Discipline makes you dangerous to them.

Story One: The Lottery Curse

Derrick hit the lottery — $10 million. Thought he was free. Bought cars, houses, parties, jewelry. No budget, no plan, no discipline.

Five years later, broke. Back in his mama's basement.

He thought money was freedom. But money without discipline is just gas poured on bad habits. It burns quick, and it leaves you with nothing but ashes.

The Math of Discipline

Let's break it down:

A dollar undisciplined → gone in seconds.

A dollar disciplined → invested, multiplied, passed down.

An hour undisciplined → scrolled away on Instagram.

An hour disciplined → builds skills, builds wealth, builds legacy.

Discipline doesn't add value. Discipline protects value. Without it, everything you build leaks away.

Case Study: Millionaires and Habits

Warren Buffet: Reads 500 pages a day. Not because it's glamorous, but because discipline compounds.

Kobe Bryant: In the gym at 4 a.m., every day, even when he was the best already.

Black Wall Street (Tulsa, 1921): Entire community thrived because of disciplined spending and group economics.

Every example of greatness has one common denominator: not talent, not luck, not resources — discipline.

Story Two: The Two Hustlers

Marcus and Tyrell started hustling at the same time. Marcus spent every flip on clothes and clubs. Tyrell reinvested into a store, into property, into skills.

Five years later, Marcus is broke. Tyrell is hiring.

Same start. Same opportunity. Different discipline.

The Street vs. Corporate Discipline

Street:

The hustler who reinvests, stays consistent, and avoids reckless spending builds empires.

The one who chases fast cars and fast women dies broke or locked up.

Corporate:

The worker who budgets, builds skills, and uses nights for their side hustle escapes.

The one who wastes weekends and lives for Friday stays stuck.

Discipline is the fork in the road.

Numbers Don't Lie

70% of lottery winners go broke in 5 years.

60% of NBA players go broke within 5 years of retiring.

40% of Americans can't cover a $400 emergency.

Not because they never had money. But because money without discipline disappears like smoke.

Story Three: The Man Who Missed His Moment

Andre got a settlement check — $200k. Thought he was rich. Bought a car, took trips, threw parties. Within 18 months, gone. No investments, no plan, no discipline.

Years later, he looked back and realized: the money wasn't his chance. The discipline he refused was.

Case Study: The Silent Wealth Builders

Immigrant families who run corner stores — discipline keeps them afloat. They save, reinvest, expand, even when the profit is small.

Black Wall Street — families reinvested into each other, building generational circulation.

Today's tech startups — founders eat ramen, live frugal, pour everything into scaling.

Discipline is the hidden engine behind every visible success.

The Trap of Undisciplined Freedom

Without discipline:

Freedom becomes addiction.

Money becomes chaos.

Power becomes corruption.

That's why so many fear success deep down. They want the fruit without planting roots. But fruit without roots rots quick.

Story Four: The Musician Who Fumbled

Jaylen got a viral hit. Millions of streams. Labels called. Checks rolled in. He thought he made it. But no discipline — spent everything, stopped recording, stopped grinding.

Within two years, forgotten. Back to Uber.

It wasn't talent he lacked. It was discipline.

Numbers Don't Lie (Again)

Compounding interest: $10/day invested with discipline → over $1 million in 40 years.

Fitness: 30 minutes a day of consistent training = stronger, healthier, longer life.

Entrepreneurship: 80% of small businesses that survive 10 years credit “consistent daily discipline” as the key.

The numbers prove it: discipline isn’t optional. It’s the foundation.

The Mis-Education of Discipline

The system teaches obedience, not discipline.

Obedience: “Do what you’re told.”

Discipline: “Do what you must, even when nobody’s watching.”

Obedience keeps you useful to others. Discipline makes you unstoppable for yourself. That’s why they never taught you the second one.

The Warning, The Story, The Lesson

The Warning:

Freedom without discipline collapses. If you don't build the muscle of consistency, everything you earn will vanish.

The Story:

A man built a small trucking company. Good clients, good money. But no discipline. Missed payments, late schedules, wasted profits. Within 3 years, gone. His trucks repossessed, his workers unemployed, his dream dead.

The Lesson:

Discipline is the bridge between potential and legacy. Without it, you're not building. You're leaking.

Closing Manifesto

Discipline ain't glamorous. It ain't sexy. It's boring. It's repetitive. But it's the only difference between a life that breaks and a life that builds.

Discipline is the alarm clock. Discipline is the budget. Discipline is the workout. Discipline is the notebook.

Everybody wants the crown. Few want the training. But without training, the crown will crush you. Without discipline, freedom will destroy you.

So if you want to be free, don't just dream. Don't just hustle. Build discipline. Because discipline is the gatekeeper of every freedom you'll ever touch.

Chapter Ten — Money: The Weapon and the Trap

Money Ain't the Goal — It's the Tool

"They told you money was freedom. But money without wisdom is another chain."

People chase money like it's salvation. They run after checks, after hours, after side hustles, believing the number in their account will finally set them free. But money ain't freedom. Money is a tool. A sword. A gun. A shield. In the right hands, it protects and builds. In the wrong hands, it destroys.

That's why most who touch it, lose it. Because they never learned money mastery. They only learned money survival.

Story One: The Tax Refund Illusion

Every February, the hood lights up. Tax season. Checks hit. People smile. New TVs, new rims, new vacations. For two months, it feels like freedom.

By April, it's gone. Bills stack. Debt returns. The cycle repeats.

That's not mastery. That's a system feeding you crumbs to keep you docile. Real mastery flips every refund into leverage. But they never taught that in school.

The Math of Mastery

Mastery starts with three numbers:

What you earn.

What you keep.

What you grow.

Most people only know the first. Few know the second. Almost none know the third. That's why they work for decades but leave nothing behind.

Case Study: Corporate Money vs. Worker Money

Corporations: Use debt as leverage. Borrow billions at 2% interest. Invest, profit, expand.

Workers: Use debt as chains. Borrow at 22% interest on credit cards. Drown.

The difference isn't opportunity. It's knowledge. The system teaches you debt as punishment. It teaches them debt as power.

Story Two: The Man Who Paid Himself

Marcus bought a $1,200 car — a real "sh*tbox." Instead of paying a bank $400 a month, he paid himself. Stacked $400 monthly in a savings account. Within two years, he had $10,000. Bought a better car cash. Kept stacking. That discipline created a personal bank.

That's mastery. That's how wealth grows quietly while others flex loudly.

Street vs. Corporate Money

Street Hustler:

Quick flips. Fast spending. Lives for today. Ends broke or locked.

Corporate Hustler:

Reinvests profits. Delays gratification. Lives for tomorrow. Ends owning.

Both handle the same dollar. One eats it. The other plants it.

Numbers Don't Lie

60% of NBA players go broke in 5 years.

40% of Americans have less than $500 in savings.

Millionaires on average save/invest 20% of income.

It ain't about how much you make. It's about how much you keep, and how much you multiply.

Story Three: The Reinvestment Flip

Keisha started braiding hair in her kitchen. Charged $50 a head. Instead of blowing the cash, she saved until she could buy chairs, then rented a small shop. Soon she had employees, charging $150 a head. Within 5 years, her income tripled.

Her clients thought she just got "lucky." But the truth was simple: she reinvested instead of flexing.

Case Study: Black Wall Street Economics

In Tulsa, money circulated within the community 19 times before leaving. That's mastery. Every dollar employed somebody. Every dollar built wealth. Compare that to today, where the average Black dollar leaves the community in 6 hours.

That's not poverty. That's leakage. And the fix isn't "more money." It's mastery.

The Budget vs. The Flex

They don't teach us budgeting because budgeting is rebellion. Every dollar tracked is a bullet aimed at the system. Because if you master money, you don't need payday loans. You don't need credit cards. You don't need debt slavery.

That's why they push flexing. New Jordans, new iPhones, new rims. They laugh because the same $300 you spent on sneakers could've bought stock in Nike. Instead of owning the shoe, you could've owned the company.

That's the difference between consumer and owner. Slave and free.

Story Four: The Two Families

Family A: Earns $50k. Saves 10%. Invests in index funds. Buys a used car cash. Lives below means. Within 20 years, net worth $500k.

Family B: Earns $100k. Spends 110%. New cars, vacations, debt. Within 20 years, net worth $0.

More income didn't mean more wealth. Mastery did.

Numbers Don't Lie (Again)

Compound interest: $300 a month invested from age 25 → $1 million by 65.

Car loans: $400/month × 30 years = $144,000 wasted on depreciating assets.

Renting vs. ownership: 30 years of rent = $400k–$600k with nothing left behind.

Mastery isn't about being rich now. It's about refusing to stay broke later.

Case Study: Fort Knox Money

Buy a cheap home. Pay it off quick. Use compound interest in a high-yield account to cover property taxes forever. That's a fortress. That's "Fort Knox money." You'll never be homeless. You'll never be fully broke. That's wealth disguised as simplicity.

Story Five: The Legacy Saver

Grandma saved $50 a month for 40 years. No flex. No vacations. Just discipline. When she passed, her grandchildren inherited $120,000.

She never made more than $30k a year. But she mastered her money. Her legacy wasn't luxury — it was stability.

The Trap of Financial Illiteracy

Financial illiteracy is the system's greatest weapon. That's why schools never taught:

How credit works.

How compound interest works.

How taxes can be avoided legally.

How to build assets instead of debts.

Because a financially literate worker is unmanageable. And an unmanageable worker is dangerous.

The Warning, The Story, The Lesson

The Warning:

If you don't master your money, your money will master you. Every dollar untracked becomes a chain. Every debt unpaid becomes a prison.

The Story:

A man made $200k a year. Big house. Fancy cars. But no discipline. Lived check to check. When the 2008 crash hit, he lost everything. His income was high, but his mastery was zero.

The Lesson:

Don’t chase more money until you master the money you already have. Because money only multiplies discipline, not wisdom.

Closing Manifesto

Money is not evil. Money is not holy. Money is neutral. It’s a weapon. The question is — who’s holding it, and how?

In the hands of the undisciplined, money is chains. In the hands of the wise, money is wings. In the hands of the selfish, money is poison. In the hands of the builder, money is freedom.

Don’t just chase it. Don’t just spend it. Master it. Because mastery of money is mastery of future. And without it, all freedom is temporary.

Chapter Eleven — Legacy: The Proof of Living

You Don't Own It Until It Outlives You

"Legacy ain't what you leave in your pocket. Legacy is what you leave in their hands."

Too many people think success is a car, a chain, a moment of flex. But success that dies with you was never success — it was entertainment. Legacy is the only scoreboard that matters. If what you built collapses when you collapse, you never built at all.

Legacy is the bridge between your life and the next life. And if you don't build it, the system already wrote your children's script: debt, struggle, obedience, silence.

Story One: The Two Funerals

Funeral A: A man dies at 67. He worked faithfully, owned nothing, left nothing. His kids cry, then return to work on Monday, still broke.

Funeral B: A man dies at 67. He wasn't rich, but he owned his house, left savings, left land. His kids cry, then plant seeds on the land he left. Their children inherit more.

Same tears. Different futures. One man died. The other man lived forever through his legacy.

The Math of Legacy

A $300,000 life insurance policy = a child who goes to college debt-free.

A $150,000 home, paid off, passed down = stability for generations.

A $10,000 investment account = a grandchild with a head start.

Legacy doesn't require millions. Legacy requires discipline, vision, and consistency.

Case Study: Black Wall Street vs. Today

In Tulsa, legacy was the air. Businesses, schools, hospitals — all built to outlive individuals. A child born in Greenwood inherited opportunity just by existing. That's legacy.

Today, the average Black family has $24k in wealth. The average White family has $188k. The gap isn't just racism. It’s the destruction of legacy and the failure to rebuild it.

The system profits off our lack of legacy. Every generation forced to start from zero is a victory for them.

Story Two: The Absent Father’s Debt

Reggie never thought about legacy. He worked, he partied, he flexed. When he died at 52, his children didn’t inherit money. They inherited debt. Funeral costs. Bills. Nothing but stress.

His name didn’t open doors. It closed them. His legacy was a burden.

Legacy isn’t optional. You leave one either way. The question is: will it feed them or starve them?

Street vs. Corporate Legacy

Street Hustler:

Buys chains, cars, women. Dies young. Kids inherit enemies and bills.

Rare hustler flips into stores, land, businesses. Kids inherit freedom.

Corporate Worker:

Works faithfully, dies with a pension check that disappears. No assets left.

Worker who invests, owns, and protects → kids inherit stability.

Both prove the same truth: loyalty alone doesn't leave legacy. Ownership does.

Numbers Don't Lie

70% of generational wealth is gone by the second generation.

90% is gone by the third.

Only 20% of African Americans have life insurance.

Less than 5% own businesses passed down.

Legacy isn't built by accident. Legacy is intentional.

Story Three: The Grandma With Land

Miss Hattie worked as a maid her whole life. Saved pennies. Bought 10 acres of land. Never sold it. When she died, her grandchildren inherited it. Developers came years later, offered millions.

That land changed the bloodline. Miss Hattie wasn't rich while alive. But her legacy fed people she never met.

Case Study: The Wealthy vs. the Working Class

Wealthy families: set up trusts, wills, foundations. Assets transfer tax-free.

Working families: die without wills. Assets lost to courts. Children inherit debt.

The system knows the difference. That's why lawyers get rich off probate, while trust funds flow silently to the next generation.

The Mis-Education of Legacy

Schools teach you to get a job. They never teach you to pass anything down.

No classes on wills.

No classes on insurance.

No classes on property law.

No classes on family banking.

Because if you master legacy, you break their cycle. And if you break their cycle, you break their control.

Story Four: The Son Who Changed the Script

Darius grew up poor. Watched his parents struggle. When he got older, he made a vow: "It stops with me." He bought insurance. Bought land. Built a business. Taught his children.

When he died, his son didn't start from zero. His son started from where Darius left off. That's the power of one generation refusing to pass down poverty.

Numbers Don't Lie (Again)

Life insurance is cheaper than cable. $40/month = $250k policy.

The average car note is $500/month. Over 30 years = $180k wasted. That's the cost of a house.

A $200/month investment at 8% return for 30 years = $270k.

Legacy isn't about being rich. It's about refusing to leave your children broke.

Case Study: The Slave Master's Legacy

Slavery ended legally in 1865. But White families passed down land, businesses, and wealth built on free labor. Those legacies still exist today. Meanwhile, our families were told: "You're free now. Good luck."

That's why the wealth gap exists. It's not just racism in the present. It's compounded legacy theft from the past. And the only way forward is to rebuild intentionally.

The Warning, The Story, The Lesson

The Warning:

If you don't build legacy, your children will inherit your cage. Poverty passed down is still a legacy — just the wrong one.

The Story:

A father worked his whole life but never owned anything. When he died, his son had to start from zero. That son worked hard but repeated the cycle. By the third generation, nobody even remembered the grandfather's struggle. His life vanished like dust.

The Lesson:

Legacy is proof you existed. If your children don't inherit anything but memories, you didn't live — you rented time. Build something that outlives you.

Closing Manifesto

Legacy is not cars. Legacy is not chains. Legacy is not clout.

Legacy is land. Legacy is knowledge. Legacy is assets. Legacy is your name opening doors long after you're gone.

Your life is not measured by what you owned while breathing. Your life is measured by what breathes after you're gone because of what you owned.

So write the will. Buy the land. Get the insurance. Teach the game. Build the legacy. Because freedom is not just about you. It's about them.

And until you build legacy, you were never free.

Chapter Twelve — Final Freedom: The Unwritten Future

Freedom Ain't a Dream — It's a Discipline

"They told you freedom was a dream. But dreams without work are hallucinations."

By now, you've seen the script: programmed from birth, institutionalized into silence, trapped in math that don't add up, starved of discipline, robbed of money mastery, stripped of legacy. The system is airtight — unless you break it.

Final freedom ain't about running from the cage. It's about burning it down so your children never see it again.

Story One: The Man With Two Lives

There was a man named Andre. He lived his first life in obedience. School, church, job, debt. At 40, he looked around and realized nothing he'd built would outlive him.

So he chose a second life. He quit. Built a business. Bought land. Wrote a book. Taught his children. When he died at 72, the first life was forgotten. The second life fed generations.

Freedom ain't about how you start. Freedom is about where you flip.

The Three Levels of Freedom

Personal Freedom: Breaking your own chains. Mastering your discipline, your money, your time.

Family Freedom: Passing down assets, knowledge, systems. Breaking generational curses.

Collective Freedom: Building communities that can't be erased. Tulsa rebuilt. ReinStone reborn.

Anything less is partial. And partial freedom is still slavery.

Case Study: Collective Wealth vs. Individual Flex

In 1921 Tulsa, 600 businesses thrived because collective freedom was the mission.

In 2025 America, individuals flex cars and clothes while communities starve.

The difference ain't opportunity. The difference is whether freedom is selfish or strategic.

Story Two: The Woman Who Refused Silence

Keisha grew up in poverty. Made it out. Got a job. Lived comfortably. But she realized her comfort didn't free her people. So she started teaching financial literacy classes in her church basement. Kids learned, families shifted, cycles broke.

Her legacy wasn't her paycheck. It was her impact.

That's final freedom — when your moves ripple beyond yourself.

Numbers Don't Lie

Black spending power: $1.6 trillion annually.

Less than 2% stays in our communities.

100 million Americans live paycheck to paycheck while corporations post record profits.

We have the money. We lack the systems. Final freedom is turning dollars into structures that can't be erased.

The Street vs. Corporate Endgame

Street:

Hustler thinks freedom is fast money. Ends dead or in chains.

Wise hustler flips into ownership, builds businesses, outlives the block.

Corporate:

Worker thinks freedom is a steady paycheck. Retires broke.

Wise worker flips into investments, side hustles, land, businesses. Leaves legacy.

Both worlds end in two choices: survival or freedom. The path is different. The law is the same.

Story Three: The Freedom Funeral

James died broke. His funeral was paid for by donations. His children mourned, then clocked back in on Monday.

Malik died with land, insurance, and businesses. His funeral was covered, his children inherited stability, his name carried weight.

Both men died. Only one man lived free.

Case Study: The Blueprint of the Builders

Madam C.J. Walker: First Black woman millionaire. Didn't just sell hair products — built distribution networks and empowered others.

Marcus Garvey: Built economic systems, not just speeches. Ships, businesses, jobs.

Nipsey Hussle: Preached ownership, practiced it. Left blueprints, not just music.

They didn't chase applause. They built freedom.

The Trap of Comfort

The most dangerous cage is the one that feels good. A steady paycheck. A safe neighborhood. A little debt but manageable.

Comfort kills revolutions. Comfort whispers: "At least you're not starving. At least you're not homeless. Stay put."

But comfort without freedom is just a padded prison.

Story Four: The Man Who Almost Built

Terrence had vision. Started a business. Made money. But instead of building legacy, he got comfortable. Bought toys. Chased women. Forgot discipline. When he died, nothing remained. His children started over.

Final freedom requires more than vision. It requires relentless building, even when you feel "safe."

Numbers Don't Lie (Again)

Every empire in history collapsed when comfort replaced discipline. Rome. Egypt. America.

80% of wealthy families lose it by the second generation.

Community ownership multiplies wealth 10x faster than individual success.

The numbers prove it: final freedom is not about you. It's about what survives without you.

The Warning, The Story, The Lesson

The Warning:

If you stop at personal success, you've built nothing. Final freedom requires building systems that live when you don't.

The Story:

A father became rich but never taught his children. When he died, they wasted it all. His freedom ended with him. Another father became stable but taught his children discipline and money mastery. When he died, they multiplied it. His freedom lived forever.

The Lesson:

Final freedom is not personal. It's generational. If your bloodline doesn't inherit, you never lived free.

Closing Manifesto

You've been programmed. Institutionalized. Trapped in math that don't add up. You've learned discipline. Mastered money. Built legacy.

Now comes the final step: writing the unwritten future.

Final freedom is not the car you drive. Not the chain you flex. Not the applause you get. Final freedom is your name echoing through generations because you built something that could not die.

So build the systems. Buy the land. Teach the children. Create the businesses. Protect the culture.

Because final freedom is not about escaping the cage. Final freedom is about making sure the cage never exists again.

BONUS CHAPTER — The Launch Pad Blueprint

"Escape takes clarity. Not just courage."

Before you jump, build your Launch Pad.

1. Good Credit (or no debt):
Gives you leverage. Even a $500 secured card can grow.

2. Reliable Vehicle:
If you can move, you can hustle. If not, partner with someone who can.

3. Emergency Savings ($500–$2,000):
Just enough to keep you calm while your business grows.

4. Low or No Bills:
Cut your lifestyle early. Freedom isn't fancy — it's focused.

5. Stacked Plans:
Have 2–3 ways to make money. If Plan A slows, Plan B runs.

6. Loan Blueprint (if you use one):
Budget that loan down to the last penny.
Leave 10–20% wiggle room for setbacks.
Never blow it fast. You're building something slow and strong.

7. Practice First.

Do 3–5 jobs, even for free, to prove your process works.

8. Confidence Kit:
One outfit. One scent. One intro speech. One pitch.
Be so prepared you feel expensive when you walk in.

9. Stay Public.
Show your journey. Even if nobody likes or shares it now.
They're watching.
And they'll circle back when it's undeniable.

10. Don't Wait for Permission.
No one's coming to crown you.
So build your own throne — and sit down.

This is your flight path from mental prison to personal power.
It's not easy.
But it's possible.
And it starts the moment you decide:

"I'm worth more than what they're paying me to forget who I am."

The People Around You: Relationships & OQP

"You can't build a kingdom surrounded by clowns."

One of the greatest tests on this journey isn't money.
It's not even skill.
It's the people you let breathe in your circle.

Your environment is either your gasoline or your slow leak. And the sad truth? Most people you love don't know how to love you once you start building.

Love Isn't Always Loyalty

You'll have family that cooked for you, housed you, prayed for you — and still, the second you say, "I'm about to change my life," they'll laugh.

Not because they hate you. But because your change is a mirror to their comfort.

You'll have friends who dapped you up every weekend, smoked with you, chased women with you — but the second you say, "I'm working on my brand tonight," they'll ghost. Not because you disrespected them. But because they realize they're standing still.

Love doesn't equal alignment.
Support doesn't equal understanding.
And loyalty doesn't equal growth.

OQP — Only Quality People

Jim Rohn said it decades ago: You are the average of the five people you spend the most time with.

But for us? It's deeper.

You need OQP — Only Quality People.

Who are they?

People who push you when you get lazy.

People who tell you the truth, not what strokes your ego.

People who clap for you without asking what's in it for them.

People who don't just want access to your shine, but will help you clean the mud off your boots on the way there.

If someone is always draining, doubting, distracting, or disrespecting? They're not OQP. They're an anchor.

And anchors don't let ships sail.

When Loneliness Hits

Here's the part most people won't tell you:
When you cut off the leeches, you'll be alone for a while.

That's the tax of elevation.

You'll eat alone. Work alone. Go to events alone. You'll feel the silence so heavy you'll want to run back to the familiar — even if the familiar was killing you.

But don't.

That silence is where you hear yourself clearly for the first time. That space is where God meets you. That solitude is where the blueprint gets written.

Relationships and Love Life

Let's keep it raw:
The wrong partner will drain more years than the wrong job.

Choose someone who:

Sees your vision and adds to it, not mocks it.

Understands sacrifice now for comfort later.

Doesn't compete with your grind, but complements it.

Loves the builder in you, not just the results.

Because nothing is worse than building your empire — and realizing the person inside your castle is sabotaging you from within.

Protect the Throne

Your life is a throne. Not everyone deserves to sit next to you.

Some deserve to watch from the crowd.
Some deserve to clap from the stands.
And a select few? They've earned the right to be on the battlefield with you.

Protect your throne with OQP.

Because once you finally make it, the wrong people will turn your palace into a prison all over again.

"They told you to chase money. They should've told you to chase the right people."

Money matters. Discipline matters. Legacy matters. But none of it survives in the wrong circle. The people around you are either multiplying your freedom or murdering it in silence. Your circle is your ceiling. If you sit with clowns, don't expect to build empires.

The system knows this. That's why it conditions you to trust the wrong ones. Friends who drain. Family who discourage. Partners who betray. Because if you waste your freedom on the wrong people, you'll destroy yourself without them lifting a finger.

Story One: The Wrong Crew

Trey had a vision. He wanted to open a car detailing business. Saved $5,000. Told his friends. They laughed. Said: "Why waste money on that? Let's hit the club, let's flip some quick cash."

He listened. Spent his savings chasing fast schemes with his crew. Lost it all. Years later, he realized the truth: it wasn't his plan that failed. It was his circle.

The Science of OQP

Dr. George Fraser, Black wealth expert, said it plain: "Surround yourself with Only Quality People (OQP)."

Why? Because environment shapes outcomes.

If 5 of your closest friends are broke, you will be the 6th.

If 5 of your closest friends are disciplined, you will be the 6th.

If 5 of your closest friends are builders, you will be the 6th.

That's not motivational fluff. That's psychology. Humans mirror their environment. And your circle is the mirror you stare into daily.

Case Study: Mastermind Groups

Andrew Carnegie, Henry Ford, Thomas Edison, Harvey Firestone — giants in different industries. But their secret weapon was their circle. They built a mastermind group, meeting often to share ideas, sharpen each other, and expand power. Together, they shaped industries. Alone, they would've been limited.

Jay-Z, Diddy, LeBron James, Maverick Carter: same principle. Billionaires, not just from skill, but from strategic circles that cross-pollinate power.

The lesson: freedom multiplies when your circle is strategic.

Story Two: The Betrayal

Monique opened a boutique. Trusted her cousin as a partner. Gave her access to money, product, accounts. Within a year, her cousin stole thousands, tanked the business, left her in debt.

She learned too late: loyalty without qualification is suicide. Blood don't equal OQP.

Street vs. Corporate Circles

Street:

Wrong circle: jealousy, betrayal, setups. Hustlers plotting on each other, ending in prison or caskets.

Right circle: loyalty, vision, collective flips. Crews that build out of the game into ownership.

Corporate:

Wrong circle: coworkers who gossip, managers who sabotage, "friends" who celebrate your failure.

Right circle: mentors, allies, partners who push you into new rooms.

Both prove the law: your circle decides your ceiling.

Numbers Don't Lie

Harvard study: Your income is the average of your five closest friends.

Addiction research: Recovery rates double when surrounded by sober, supportive circles.

Wealth stats: 85% of self-made millionaires credit "strategic relationships" as the key.

The math is simple: your circle predicts your future.

Story Three: The Hidden Hater

Devon finally started his business. Excited, he told his best friend. Instead of support, his friend mocked him. Said: “Man, you think you better than us?”

Months later, Devon realized that “friend” never once shared his flyers, never once referred a client, never once supported.

A friend who won’t clap for you in public is an enemy in disguise. That’s the price of the wrong circle.

Case Study: Tulsa vs. Today

In 1921 Greenwood (Black Wall Street), OQP wasn’t just individuals — it was community. Business owners fed into each other. Dollars circled 19 times before leaving.

Today, wrong circles drain money in hours. We flex for clout, compete with friends, spend with outsiders, and wonder why we’re still broke.

Legacy was never just destroyed by bombs. It was destroyed by broken circles.

The Circle and Discipline

Discipline alone ain't enough if your circle mocks it. If you're trying to save but your crew spends, you'll fold. If you're trying to build but your crew parties, you'll stall.

Your circle decides whether your discipline survives or dies.

Story Four: The Elevator Test

Lisa wanted to level up. She started hanging with mentors, going to conferences, joining rooms above her income bracket. At first, she felt small. But slowly, her mindset shifted.

Within 5 years, her income tripled. Same Lisa. Different circle.

The Warning, The Story, The Lesson

The Warning:

Your circle can kill your freedom quicker than poverty. Poverty can be escaped. A wrong circle will drag you back into it.

The Story:

A hustler stacked $50k. Told his crew. They convinced him to blow it on cars and chains. Within months, broke again. Years later, he admitted: "It wasn't the system that robbed me. It was the people I trusted."

The Lesson:

OQP is not optional. It's survival. Protect your circle like you protect your money. Because the wrong people will spend both.

Closing Manifesto

Your circle is your ceiling. Your friends are your future. Your environment is your inheritance.

Stop begging clowns to clap for you. Stop trusting leeches with your vision. Stop mistaking blood for loyalty. Freedom requires OQP — Only Quality People. Build with them, protect them, sharpen them. Because without the right circle, you'll never break the cage.

And when you find OQP, you'll realize freedom was never just about you. It was about us.

Bonus Chapter Two Health as Wealth

"You can't build a kingdom with a broken body."

We talk money like it's everything.

But what good is $10,000 in the bank if you can't walk up the stairs without losing your breath?

What good is freedom if your body collapses before you taste it?

They programmed us to grind, not to heal.

To push until the back gives out, until the teeth rot, until the stomach burns from stress.

And then they sell us pills as if disease is the normal price of being alive.

But hear me: health is the first form of wealth.

If you don't protect it, everything else is temporary.

The Real Cost of Neglect

It's not just obesity.

It's diabetes. Hypertension. Heart disease. Tooth decay. Depression.

Black men and women dying ten years earlier than they should — not because we're weaker, but because we've been taught to ignore ourselves until it's too late.

You'll work 40 years, retire at 65, and spend the rest of your life in doctor's offices.

That's not living. That's leasing your life to sickness.

Discipline Is Sacred

You don't need a six-pack. You need stamina.

You don't need to look like a model. You need mobility.

You don't need to run marathons. You need energy when your kids say, "Come play with me."

Health isn't about vanity. It's about victory.

The discipline to:

Drink water instead of soda.

Cook real food instead of fast food.

Stretch in the morning instead of rolling straight into chaos.

Put the blunt or the bottle down sometimes and let your body breathe.

Discipline is sacred because your body is your temple. And if your temple collapses, the whole kingdom falls with it.

Dental, Mental, and Daily

Don't just think gym. Think whole body.

Dental: You can't smile with confidence if your teeth are rotting. Invest in your mouth.

Mental: Therapy, journaling, meditation — whatever keeps your head clear. A stressed mind will kill you faster than a bad diet.

Daily: Walks. Pushups. Drinking a gallon of water. Small things stacked daily turn into long life.

Stop waiting until you're in pain to care.

That's not health. That's damage control.

Freedom Is No Fun If You're Sick

Picture this: you built the business. You made the money. You escaped the job.

But you can't enjoy it because your knees are shot, your teeth ache, your heart is weak, your lungs are gone.

That's not freedom.

That's slavery to your body.

The real win is being 50 years old, strong enough to run, laugh, travel, and still grind like you're 30.

That's wealth.

Health = Leverage

When you walk into a room healthy, sharp, glowing, smelling good, body upright — people respect you before you speak.

When you record content with energy, your audience feels it.

When you're on the grind, you can outlast everybody because your body is trained for it.

That's why health is leverage.

Not just for life — but for business, relationships, and legacy.

Protect the Vessel

You only get one body.

Treat it like the million-dollar machine it is.

Because the truth is…

You can replace money.

You can rebuild a business.

You can repair a brand.

But you can't trade in your lungs.

You can't buy another heart.

You can't reset time.

Protect the vessel.

Because once it breaks, the game is over.

"They told you to chase money. They should've told you to guard your health."

You can't build freedom in a broken body. You can't pass down legacy if you don't live long enough to protect it. You can't fight systems if you're too sick to stand.

But here's the trap: America profits off your sickness. Food, hospitals, insurance, pharmaceuticals — billion-dollar industries designed to keep you alive just enough to work, but never well enough to thrive.

That's why protecting your body isn't just personal. It's spiritual. It's economic. It's revolutionary.

Story One: The Worker Who Collapsed

Jamal was 42. Worked double shifts at the plant. Drank sodas for energy, smoked cigarettes for stress, ate fast food for convenience. One day, he collapsed on the line. Heart attack. Dead before the ambulance arrived.

The company sent flowers. His family got nothing. His body was the business. And when it failed, the business replaced him in 24 hours.

That's how the system eats: on your back, your lungs, your heart.

The Math of Sickness

Medical bankruptcies: 66% of bankruptcies in America are caused by medical debt.

Fast food: $200 billion industry, feeding obesity, diabetes, and cancer.

Pharma: Over $500 billion annually in U.S. drug sales — many drugs for diseases caused by lifestyle.

Your sickness is their profit. Your pain is their dividend.

Case Study: The Dental Trap

They don't tell you this: poor dental health is linked to heart disease, stroke, and even Alzheimer's.

But the dental industry is designed to bleed you. Root canal? $1,200–$2,500. Crown? $1,000+. Braces? $5,000–$7,000. Insurance rarely covers more than scraps.

Now picture the worker at $17/hr. One broken tooth is a month of wages. That's why millions walk around with missing teeth — not because they don't care, but because the math don't math.

And that broken smile affects jobs, self-esteem, relationships. The system knows it. That's why they profit twice: once from your pain, again from your poverty.

Story Two: The Fast Food Funeral

Keisha fed her kids McDonald's five nights a week. It was cheap, quick, easy. At 52, she was diagnosed with diabetes. By 58, she was gone.

Her children inherited grief and bills. That's legacy stolen by processed food. And those companies knew exactly what they were doing.

Street vs. Corporate Health

Street Hustler Health:

Stress, bad food, cigarettes, late nights. Dies young, legacy erased.

Corporate Worker Health:

Stress, fast food lunches, sitting 8 hours, no exercise. Dies early, legacy erased.

Different uniforms. Same death. Same profit for the system.

Numbers Don't Lie

Black men: Life expectancy is 7 years shorter than White men.

Heart disease: #1 killer in America. Preventable with diet, exercise, and stress management.

Obesity: 42% of Americans are obese. Linked to $147 billion in annual healthcare costs.

They're not killing us with bullets alone. They're killing us with burgers, pills, and stress.

Story Three: The Prison Body

Dante went to prison at 19. Ate processed meals, little movement. By 30, he had high blood pressure. By 40, diabetes. By 45, dead.

Prison didn't just take his freedom. It took his health. And that was the plan. Because a sick body is a silent body.

Case Study: The Gym Prescription

Did you know doctors can prescribe gym memberships in some states? That tells you everything. They know movement is medicine. But instead of promoting prevention, they sell pills. Because pills pay. Gyms don't.

The system knows the cure. It just ain't profitable.

The Temple Within

Your body is the temple. The temple of God. The temple of legacy. The temple of every dream. And temples ain't maintained by accident. They're maintained with discipline.

Fasting to clean the body.

Exercise to strengthen it.

Real food to fuel it.

Rest to restore it.

The same way you invest in businesses, you must invest in your flesh. Because a broken temple can't hold freedom.

Story Four: The Turnaround

Lisa weighed 260 pounds. Always tired. Always stressed. One day, her doctor told her: "If you don't change, you'll be gone by 50."

She started walking daily. Cut soda. Cooked meals. Lost 80 pounds. Gained energy. Started a small business with her new fire.

Her children didn't just inherit her money. They inherited her discipline. That's legacy.

Numbers Don't Lie (Again)

Every pound lost reduces joint stress by 4 pounds.

30 minutes of walking daily cuts risk of heart disease by 50%.

Every $1 spent on prevention saves $3 in medical costs.

Health is not just survival. It's economics.

The Trap of Stress

Stress kills silently.

Raises blood pressure.

Weakens immunity.

Fuels strokes and heart attacks.

And what fuels stress? Workplaces. Bills. Poverty. Oppression. The system profits twice: once off your labor, again off your sickness.

Case Study: Corporate Food Manipulation

Corn syrup subsidies: Billions spent to keep junk food cheap.

Pharma lobbying: Billions spent to keep prescriptions high.

Food deserts: Black neighborhoods left without healthy options, flooded with fast food.

This ain't accident. It's strategy.

The Warning, The Story, The Lesson

The Warning:

If you don't guard your health, your body will collapse before your dreams bloom. And the system will profit from both your labor and your death.

The Story:

A man worked 30 years, saved money, built a business. But he never cared for his health. At 55, a stroke ended him. His business died with him. His children inherited nothing but stress.

The Lesson:

Freedom requires a healthy body. Health is not optional. It's the first wealth. Without it, money is meaningless, legacy is lost, and freedom is fantasy.

Closing Manifesto

Health is wealth. Your body is the first asset. Your lungs, your heart, your teeth, your back — they are worth more than any chain, any car, any house.

Guard your body like you guard your money. Build your body like you build your business. Protect your body like you protect your children. Because health is not just survival. Health is revolution.

Eat clean. Move daily. Rest deeply. Fast often. Because every day you invest in your temple, you invest in freedom.

And without a strong temple, no empire will ever stand.

Legacy & Community

"You can be rich alone. But you can't build a nation by yourself."

The lie they sold us was independence without interdependence.

They told us, "Go get yours. Stack for yourself. Flex on the next man."

But real legacy ain't in flexing.

It's in building something that breathes after you're gone.

Money Dies. Legacy Doesn't.

A car loses value the moment you drive it off the lot.

Clothes fade.

Watches get scratched.

Even businesses can fold.

But legacy?

Legacy outlives your name.

Legacy is when your kids don't have to choose between rent and food.

Legacy is when a community grows fruit from the trees you planted.

Legacy is when your name is whispered with respect, even when nobody alive ever met you.

Why Legacy Is Group Work

One man can start a business.

One woman can raise a child.

But legacy takes a tribe.

It takes neighbors who trust each other.

It takes families who pour into the same pot.

It takes a vision bigger than your own survival.

Because survival makes you selfish.

But legacy makes you generous.

You start asking:

What happens after me?

Who eats when I'm gone?

What do my people inherit besides bills and trauma?

Building Beyond Yourself

Legacy doesn't start with millions. It starts with movement.

A group of men all buying land together.

A circle of women pooling money to fund a school.

Neighbors watching each other's kids so no one falls behind.

Small collective moves become cultural monuments.

Don't just buy sneakers. Buy soil.

Don't just show off jewelry. Show off schools.

Don't just post selfies. Post solutions.

Because what you flex fades.

But what you build feeds.

The Currency of Community

Your money isn't the only wealth.

Time: When you mentor a kid, you give years back to the future.

Skill: When you teach somebody a trade, you multiply their earning power.

Energy: When you show up consistently, you create trust that no loan can buy.

Community thrives on currencies the bank doesn't recognize.

And when those currencies circulate?

Poverty has no power.

Legacy Is Insurance

Life is unpredictable.

Cars crash. Teeth crack. Jobs fold.

But when you have community, you're never bankrupt.

Because legacy is insurance.

It guarantees that when one person falls, ten hands are waiting to lift them.

And when those ten hands fall, a hundred hands are behind them.

That's how you break cycles.

That's how you outlive systems designed to bury you.

From Brand to Blueprint

Understand this: your personal brand isn't just about you.

It's the first brick in the foundation.

The content you make inspires.

The business you build funds.

The wealth you stack seeds.

The network you form multiplies.

And little by little, you move from one man's vision… to a blueprint for a thousand.

Because at the end of the day, being rich is nice.

But leaving your people richer?

That's immortality.

"They told you to get permission. But business don't ask. Business moves."

We've been programmed to believe business requires credentials. An MBA. A loan. A partner with connections. They want you thinking you need approval before you can eat.

But the truth is blunt: the most successful hustlers didn't wait. They didn't ask. They moved. Business is not a classroom. Business is the street. And every lesson you need is outside, waiting.

Story One: The Lemonade Hustle

A little girl in Chicago set up a lemonade stand. Didn't know marketing. Didn't know accounting. But she knew hustle. Smiled, waved, sold cups. By the end of summer, she had $400.

That was her MBA. Real movement, real customers, real feedback.

Now ask yourself: how many adults with degrees never built anything real? That's the difference between permission and action.

The Myth of the MBA

Cost of an MBA: $60,000–$200,000.

Average debt: $66,000.

Average salary after graduation: $115,000.

Meanwhile, most entrepreneurs build with less than $5,000 in startup money. They learn faster, fail faster, pivot faster.

The system wants you chasing paper while they chase profit. But business mastery comes from motion, not diplomas.

Case Study: Ray Kroc vs. the McDonald Brothers

McDonald brothers had the product. Burgers, fries, fast service.

Ray Kroc had the hustle. Franchised, marketed, scaled.

He didn't invent. He multiplied.

That's business without permission. He saw the play and ran it while others hesitated.

Story Two: The Corner Flip

DeShawn started with $200. Bought cleaning supplies. Knocked on doors offering house cleaning. Some slammed doors. Some laughed. But three said yes. He reinvested. Bought uniforms. Bought a van. Within 5 years, he had a cleaning company making six figures.

No degree. No permission. Just hustle.

The Hustler's MBA Curriculum

Forget Harvard. Here's the real curriculum:

Sales 101: Knock on doors. Cold call. Pitch strangers.

Marketing 101: Pass out flyers. Post content. Build buzz.

Finance 101: Track every dollar. Reinvest first. Eat last.

Leadership 101: Hire slow. Fire fast. Lead by example.

Resilience 101: Fail, adjust, return stronger.

Every hustler already has the skills. The streets taught them. The job taught them. The pain taught them. The only difference is whether you apply it to ownership.

Street vs. Corporate Business

Street Hustle:

Limited resources. High risk. Creative flips.

No lawyers, no accountants, just survival.

One bad move = jail.

Corporate Hustle:

Unlimited resources. Risk spread. Creative loopholes.

Lawyers, accountants, lobbyists.

One bad move = bailout.

Same energy. Different protection. The hustler's mistake is thinking he's not qualified. But the truth is: he's been running businesses his whole life — just without paperwork.

Numbers Don't Lie

Average Black-owned business starts with $35,000 less capital than White-owned businesses.

But 50% of side hustles scale into full businesses within 3 years.

Over 60% of millionaires are self-made entrepreneurs.

The numbers prove: you don't need credentials. You need consistency.

Story Three: The Vendor Who Outran Walmart

Maria started selling tamales from her kitchen. Word spread. Soon, lines around the block. Walmart tried to undercut. But her brand was personal. Her customers were loyal. She scaled into restaurants.

She didn't wait for a business loan. She didn't wait for investors. She built from stove to empire. That's the Hustler's MBA.

Case Study: Nipsey Hussle — All Money In

Nipsey didn't beg labels. He sold CDs out the trunk. Built his own store. Branded his own marathon. Labels came later, but on his terms.

That's business without permission. That's blueprint.

The Trap of Waiting

Most people never start because they're waiting.

Waiting for the perfect idea.

Waiting for funding.

Waiting for validation.

Meanwhile, somebody else is moving with less than you, slower than you, dumber than you — and winning. Because movement beats waiting every time.

Story Four: The Barber With a Vision

Anthony cut hair in his garage. Saved. Bought chairs. Opened a shop. Expanded into three shops.

One day, he went back to his old job at Walmart — the same job he quit years ago. He realized the managers were still there, still broke, still waiting for promotions.

He didn't wait. That was the difference.

Numbers Don't Lie (Again)

Most small businesses start with less than $5k.

50% of entrepreneurs never take loans.

90% of skills needed for business are free on the internet.

Waiting is an excuse. Building is the cure.

The Hustler's MBA Lessons

Start with what you have.

Reinvest, don't flex.

Fail fast, adjust faster.

Build brand as you build product.

Don't wait for permission.

The Warning, The Story, The Lesson

The Warning:

If you wait for permission, you'll die waiting. The system never gives permission for freedom.

The Story:

A man dreamed of opening a food truck. Spent 15 years talking, researching, waiting for loans. Meanwhile, another man started with a grill on the corner. Ten years later, he owned trucks. The dreamer is still waiting.

The Lesson:

Start now. Build small. Move with what you have. Because freedom is never granted. It's built without permission.

Closing Manifesto

Business is not theory. Business is not credentials. Business is not paperwork.

Business is motion. Business is risk. Business is ownership.

The Hustler's MBA is not a diploma. It's a scar. It's a failure survived. It's a client won. It's a dollar reinvested. It's a vision built in the face of doubt.

Don’t wait for classrooms. Don’t wait for banks. Don’t wait for applause. Start where you stand. Flip what you have. Build what you need.

Because the real MBA ain’t in Harvard. It’s in your hustle.

Discipline & Daily Systems

"Freedom without discipline is just chaos in a new outfit."

Most people fail not because they lack talent, but because they lack a system.

They think motivation is enough. But motivation is a spark — discipline is the engine.

You can be gifted, passionate, even divinely inspired. But if your day is sloppy, your results will be sloppy too.

Why Systems Matter

The world doesn't reward effort. It rewards results.

And results don't come from random bursts of work.

They come from repeated, structured execution.

That's why you can see people less talented than you surpass you.

They had discipline.

They had consistency.

They had a system.

Talent without a schedule is wasted genius.

The Power of the Morning

How you start your day sets the tone for everything.

If the first thing you do is scroll, you just fed your mind junk food.

But if the first thing you do is move — stretch, write, pray, plan — you tell the day who's in charge.

Your mornings should look like:

Silence before chaos.

Vision before distraction.

Work before the world pulls you.

Start the day with your hands on your dream — not their feed.

Time Blocking: Protect Your Energy

Don't work until you're tired. Work until the block ends.

Give yourself dedicated slots:

Creation Block: Writing, filming, producing — no phone, no noise.

Admin Block: Emails, bills, invoices — get it all done in one window.

Study Block: Learning new skills, reading, sharpening the blade.

Rest Block: Yes, rest is a system too. No rest = no clarity.

When you block time, you stop leaking energy all over the place.

Discipline is a Muscle

Don't think you either "have it" or you don't.

Discipline grows the more you use it.

Start with 20 minutes of focused work.

Build to an hour.

Build to three.

Before you know it, you can run a 10-hour grind day because your mental endurance is trained.

And here's the truth: discipline is more addictive than dopamine.

Once you see what consistency does, quitting won't even feel like an option.

Cut the Leaks

Discipline isn't just about what you do. It's about what you stop doing.

People who waste your time.

Apps that eat your focus.

Habits that drain your money.

Excuses that feel good but kill progress.

Cut the leaks, and suddenly you'll feel like you gained 10 hours and $1,000 a week.

Build Rituals, Not Just Routines

Routines can feel robotic. Rituals feel sacred.

Don't just "film content."

Light your incense. Put on your scent. Play your focus music. Enter the zone.

Don't just "work out."

Make the gym your battlefield. Pray before the set. Leave sweat like an offering.

Rituals turn discipline into devotion.

And devotion makes you unstoppable.

Discipline = Freedom

The irony is this:

Most people avoid discipline because they think it's restrictive.

But the opposite is true.

Without discipline, you're a slave to your moods, cravings, and distractions.

With discipline, you're free to build anything.

Discipline is the ultimate rebellion.

It's telling the system: "I won't waste my life."

Because success isn't built on one big move.

It's built on 1,000 small moves done with precision.

Every day.

Even when nobody's watching.

Especially when nobody's watching.

That's how kings are made.

Money Management & Multiplication

"Money is not the goal. It's the fuel."

Most people get money and spend it like it's a trophy.

But money ain't a trophy — it's a tool.

If you treat it like a celebration, it disappears.

If you treat it like a seed, it multiplies.

The system already designed poverty for you. If you finally break out and make some income, the worst thing you can do is hand it right back to them through lifestyle inflation and bad habits.

Why Most People Stay Broke After the Breakthrough

Because they thought money was freedom by itself.

It's not.

Money with no plan is just chaos with a price tag.

That's why you see people get raises, bonuses, even settlements — and five years later they're back where they started.

They upgraded their car. Their clothes. Their phone. Their bills.

They didn't upgrade their strategy.

First Rule: Control the Flow

Every dollar you make needs a home before you spend it.

Necessities (50%): Rent, food, car, insurance — the basics that keep you alive.

Freedom Fund (30%): Business investments, savings, loan payoff, equipment. This is the money that buys your exit.

Flex (20%): Entertainment, clothes, enjoyment — because you still need to live.

This ain't a strict law, but it's a blueprint. The point is: you don't spend first and think later. You assign first, then spend.

Second Rule: Eliminate Chains Early

Debt is the modern plantation.

Every interest payment is rent on your freedom.

So you kill it. Not slowly. Aggressively.

Triple up on payments. Use side hustle money to cut the balance. Treat debt like an enemy, not a roommate.

The faster you clear it, the lighter your life gets.

Third Rule: Multiply With Discipline

Once you free up money, you don't throw it at every opportunity. You invest with clarity.

Skills: Courses, mentors, books — the ROI on knowledge lasts forever.

Assets: Equipment that makes you money, not drains it. Cameras, tools, land, businesses.

Networks: Events, travel, spaces where the right conversations happen. One connection can out-earn a year's salary.

Savings Vehicles: High-yield accounts, Roth IRAs, community investment pools.

Don't gamble. Don't chase trends. Build a foundation.

The "Fort Knox" Method

Your money isn't free until your basics are protected.

Buy a cheap, solid property.

Pay it off slow but steady.

Use compound interest from a savings account to cover yearly taxes.

Result? You can never be fully evicted again.

That's Fort Knox — a base you and your bloodline can always fall back on.

Stop the Leaks

Ask yourself: Who’s eating off me?

The subscription you forgot about.

The “flex” outfit that doesn’t bring clients.

The fast food run that adds up to hundreds.

Plug the leaks. Redirect the flow. Suddenly, you’ve got money you didn’t even know you had.

The Truth About Flexing

There’s nothing wrong with looking good. But flex at the wrong time and you’ll kill your momentum.

Rich people buy time.

Poor people buy image.

Buy assets first. Buy presentation second. Buy flex last.

Because when your assets are feeding you, your flex never hurts you.

Wealth Is a System, Not a Salary

Money is not about how much you make in a week.

It's about how much you keep, how much you grow, and how much keeps working while you sleep.

The real rich don't have more hours in the day. They have more soldiers in the field — every dollar is an employee.

So stop being a spender.

Stop being a slave to wages.

Start being an owner.

Start being a general.

Because at the end of the day, money itself is not freedom.

But it is the key.

And if you learn how to control it, multiply it, and aim it…

You'll never be locked out again.

Bonus Chapter — The Digital Trap: Social Media as Prison or Platform (Expanded Edition)

The New Chains Don't Clink

"They took the chains off your hands. Then they put them on your eyes."

We talk about slavery like it ended. But the new slavery doesn't look like whips or plantations. It looks like timelines, likes, and scrolls. The new overseer is the algorithm. The new plantation is your screen. And the new cotton is your attention.

Social media is the trap of our generation — unless you flip it into your weapon.

Story One: The Scroller Who Lost Years

Darius was smart. Funny. Creative. But every night, instead of building, he scrolled. Memes, reels, gossip blogs. Hours gone. Years passed. His ideas never saw light because his energy died in the scroll.

At 35, he looked back and realized he had given Instagram more hours than he gave his own dreams. His hands were free. His body was free. But his mind? Caged.

The Science of Addiction

Every notification gives you a dopamine hit.

Every scroll is engineered to keep you hooked.

Platforms test your habits to keep you online longer.

You think you're choosing. You're not. You're programmed.

That's why TikTok knows what you like before you do. That's why Instagram never ends. That's why Twitter thrives on anger. The more you scroll, the more they profit.

Case Study: The Billion-Dollar Business of Attention

Facebook/Meta made $134 billion in ad revenue in 2023.

TikTok made $20 billion.

YouTube made $31 billion.

They don't sell products. They sell you. Every second you scroll is a dollar in their pocket. Your attention is the new oil.

Story Two: The Lost Hustler

Tyrone wanted to start a clothing brand. Followed influencers for "motivation." But instead of building, he kept comparing. Saw people flexing cars, jewelry, "overnight success." Thought he wasn't ready. Thought he needed more money, more time.

He didn't realize half of it was fake — rented cars, staged content, lies. By the time he figured it out, his confidence was gone. The trap wasn't poverty. The trap was the screen.

Street vs. Corporate Social Media

Street:

Scrolls for entertainment. Laughs, memes, gossip.

Becomes consumer. Wastes time. No legacy built.

Corporate:

Posts to build brand. Runs ads. Collects data.

Becomes owner. Sells to millions. Legacy built.

Same platform. Different use. One is prisoner. One is free.

Numbers Don't Lie

Average American spends 2.5 hours a day on social media. That's 912 hours a year — almost 38 full days.

By 70, that's 7 years of life spent scrolling.

Meanwhile, 80% of small businesses credit social media for growth.

The math is simple: the screen is either your prison or your platform.

Story Three: The Woman Who Flipped It

Keisha used to scroll TikTok all day. Then one day she said: "If I'm gonna spend hours here, I might as well get paid."

She started posting hair tutorials. At first, 50 views. Then 500. Then 5,000. Within a year, she had clients booking daily. Social media went from her prison to her billboard.

Case Study: Corporate Influence

Cambridge Analytica: Used Facebook data to manipulate elections.

TikTok: China limits kids to 40 minutes/day of educational content. In America, they let kids scroll unlimited dances, drama, and poison.

Instagram: Studies show teen depression rose 70% after Instagram's growth.

Social media isn't neutral. It's a weapon. The question is whether you're holding it or it's holding you.

The Trap of Comparison

Comparison kills more dreams than failure.

You see influencers living fake lives.

You feel small.

You stall.

Meanwhile, they profit off your envy. They flex for attention. You feed them with your time.

Freedom comes when you realize: most of it is lies. And even if it's real, it don't matter. Build your own lane.

Story Four: The Silent Builder

Malik started posting his workouts. No clout. No likes. No buzz. But he kept posting. Six months in, a gym owner called. Offered him a partnership. He never went viral. He never chased clout. He built quietly until opportunity knocked.

That's the platform mindset.

Numbers Don't Lie (Again)

Influencer marketing is a $21 billion industry.

Brands pay micro-influencers $100–$500 per post.

Top influencers make millions annually.

The same platforms that distract you can feed you — if you stop consuming and start producing.

The Rules of Flipping Social Media

Post more than you scroll.

Build brand, not clout.

Teach, entertain, inspire — never just flex.

Turn followers into clients.

Remember: you are the product, not the platform.

The Warning, The Story, The Lesson

The Warning:

If you don't control your screen, your screen will control you. The trap is invisible, but it's stealing your years.

The Story:

A man scrolled every night after work. Laughed, commented, shared. Ten years later, he was in the same job, same apartment, same struggles. He looked back and realized he gave a decade to Instagram for free.

The Lesson:

Social media is either your overseer or your stage. Use it to build, or it will use you to feed others.

Closing Manifesto

The new chains don't clink. They glow. They vibrate. They scroll.

Your attention is your freedom. Guard it. Flip it. Weaponize it. Don't let your years leak into a screen that pays you nothing. The phone in your hand is either your prison or your platform. Choose.

Post with purpose. Build with discipline. Flip the trap into a stage. Because the scroll can either bury you or build you. And freedom only comes when you take the controls back.

Bonus Chapter The Power of Image & Presence

"They see you before they hear you. So what are you saying without words?"

Before you open your mouth, your presence has already spoken.

Your clothes, your walk, your tone, your scent — all of it is part of your brand.

People buy certainty. And presence is the packaging of certainty.

Wardrobe as Armor

When you step into a room, you're either the hunted or the hunter. Your wardrobe decides which one.

A sharp turtleneck, tailored coat, clean pants, and polished shoes: you look like a man with direction.

A wrinkled hoodie, dirty sneakers, or sagging jeans: you look like a man looking for permission.

You don't need Gucci. You need discipline.

Presentation is not about labels — it's about precision.

When your look is tight, you carry yourself different. And that difference is felt before a word leaves your lips.

Grooming as Respect

If you don't take care of yourself, why should anyone trust you to take care of business?

Hair: kept, braided, lined, or locs tight.

Beard: shaped, brushed, intentional.

Skin: moisturized, glowing, cared for.

Breath: clean. No excuses.

It's not vanity. It's respect.

Respect for the people you meet. Respect for the opportunity you're chasing. Respect for the fact that every second someone spends with you is an investment.

Scent as Memory

Your smell lingers longer than your words.

A bold cologne, placed right, can become your silent trademark.

People might forget what you pitched.

They won't forget how you made them feel.

And scent is memory.

Pick one signature fragrance. Make it yours. Walk into a room, and leave with them wondering who you are.

Posture and Voice

A slouched back, rushed speech, eyes darting around — that's insecurity on display.

But stand tall. Shoulders wide. Breathe slow. Speak with pauses. Look people dead in the eye.

Now you've shifted the room. You've taken authority without shouting. You've commanded respect without asking.

Presence is not about being loud. It's about being undeniable.

Why Image Is Survival

Here's the truth:

You can have the best product, the best book, the best skill — but if your presence is weak, nobody listens.

Because the world doesn't buy what you're selling.

It buys what you're showing.

And if you show chaos, they assume your business is chaos.

If you show strength, they assume your business is strong.

That's why image matters. That's why presence matters.

Because whether you like it or not, perception is currency.

Becoming the Walking Brand

Everywhere you go, you're marketing.

Not just on Instagram. Not just when you film a reel. Everywhere.

The grocery store clerk. The gas station attendant. The random stranger you ask to hold a camera.

Each one is watching. Each one is deciding who you are.

So become intentional.

Become precise.

Become the billboard.

Because before they ever buy your product, they're buying you.

Because in this world, your presence is the down payment, your product is the proof, and your consistency is the contract.

Bonus Chapter— The Art of Rejection: Fuel for Flight

Rejection Ain't Death — It's Rent

"They told you rejection was failure. They never told you rejection was the fee for freedom."

Every dream costs something. And the price ain't just money, sweat, or time. The real price is rejection. Every builder pays it. Every hustler pays it. Every visionary pays it.

The problem is, most of us treat rejection like it's death. We fold after the first no. We run home after the first laugh. We stop knocking after the first slammed door. But rejection ain't a coffin. Rejection is rent. And rent must be paid if you want to live free.

Story One: The Door Slam

Darius wanted to sell his cleaning service. Walked into 10 offices in one day. Nine slammed the door. One receptionist laughed in his face.

He almost quit. But on office #10, someone said yes. That yes turned into a $50,000 contract.

Looking back, he realized the truth: the no's weren't wasted. They were toll booths. Each no was just a step toward the yes that mattered.

The Psychology of "No"

Rejection feels like pain because your brain treats it like danger. Evolution says: if your tribe rejects you, you die. But in business, rejection doesn't kill you — it strengthens you.

Every no desensitizes your fear. Every rejection sharpens your pitch. Every failure rewires your courage.

The ones who survive aren't the ones who never hear no. They're the ones who hear no so many times it loses power.

Case Study: Oprah Winfrey

Oprah was told she wasn't fit for television. Too raw. Too unpolished. Fired from her first TV job. That rejection became fuel. She built a style nobody could deny.

Today, she's one of the most influential women in history. The rejection wasn't her end. It was her edge.

Story Two: The Rapper With 1,000 No's

Jamal passed out mixtapes in the mall. Got clowned, ignored, brushed off. Out of 1,000, only 50 listened. Out of 50, 10 came back. Out of 10, one knew a DJ. That DJ introduced him to a producer.

The rejection wasn't wasted. It filtered the crowd until he found the one yes that mattered.

Street vs. Corporate Rejection

Street Hustler:

Knock doors, pitch product, face paranoia.

Learns that 9 no's mean nothing if the 10th yes pays the bills.

Corporate Entrepreneur:

Cold emails, investor pitches, client meetings.

Learns the average sale takes 7–12 touches.

Both worlds teach the same law: rejection is the down payment for opportunity.

Numbers Don't Lie

Walt Disney was rejected 302 times before someone funded Disney World.

Colonel Sanders was rejected over 1,000 times before KFC took off.

J.K. Rowling was rejected by 12 publishers before Harry Potter.

Sales data: Average close rate is 20%. That means 80% rejection is normal.

Rejection ain't the exception. It's the expectation.

Story Three: The Job Hunter Who Pivoted

Keisha applied for 100 jobs. Got rejected 90 times. Out of frustration, she started freelancing. Within 2 years, she made more than any of those jobs would've paid.

The rejections were redirection. The no's forced her into ownership.

Case Study: Corporate Use of Rejection

Corporations reject ideas daily. Not because they hate them — but because testing costs money. They let startups take the risk. If the idea wins, they buy it. If it fails, they saved money.

Rejection, in their world, is strategy. They filter until only proven winners remain.

Builders must think the same way. Rejection ain't failure. It's filtration.

The Trap of Thin Skin

Thin skin is poverty's best friend. If one insult, one laugh, one no can stop you, then you'll never eat free.

The system trained you to crave approval. Gold stars in school. Likes on posts. Compliments from bosses. That programming makes rejection feel fatal. But the hustler's cure is desensitization: seek rejection until it stops hurting.

Story Four: The Salesman's Game

Andre made a game of rejection. Every day, he aimed for 20 no's. He tracked them on a chart. Funny thing? By chasing no's, he got yeses. Lots of them. Because no longer fearing rejection freed him to move without shame.

Numbers Don't Lie (Again)

It takes 7–12 contacts before a yes.

Most salespeople quit after 2 contacts.

That means 90% of opportunity dies in fear of rejection.

The ones who win aren't the most talented. They're the most persistent.

Story Five: The Comic on Stage

Malik bombed his first 10 comedy sets. Crowds booed. Jokes fell flat. But he kept showing up. By the 11th, he found his rhythm. Years later, he was headlining shows.

The no's weren't setbacks. They were training.

Case Study: Thomas Edison

Edison failed 10,000 times before inventing the lightbulb. Reporters asked: "How did you keep going?" He said: "I didn't fail 10,000 times. I discovered 10,000 ways that didn't work."

Rejection was his teacher. Without it, there is no light.

The Art of Rejection

Redefine it. No isn't failure. No is rent.

Desensitize. Seek rejection until it loses sting.

Filter. Rejection shows who's not your customer, not your destiny.

Redirect. Each no pushes you closer to the lane that fits.

Fuel. Let rejection sharpen you instead of silence you.

The Warning, The Story, The Lesson

The Warning:

If rejection scares you, poverty will own you. Fear of no keeps you from every yes that matters.

The Story:

A man wanted to start a gym. Pitched investors. Got rejected 20 times. Quit. Years later, someone else opened the same concept — and thrived. His fear of rejection cost him millions.

The Lesson:

Rejection is not punishment. It's preparation. Learn to pay it gladly, because every no is rent money for freedom.

Bonus Chapter— The Shadow War: How They Profit Off Your Pain

Your Suffering is Someone's Salary

"They don't need you dead. They need you bleeding slow."

You think pain is personal. You think your stress, your sickness, your bills are just your burden. But the truth is darker: your pain is an economy. Every tear, every late payment, every pill swallowed, every pound gained — it all prints profit for someone else.

This is the shadow war. Not fought with guns, but with contracts, commercials, credit reports, and cravings. And in this war, your suffering is the resource.

Story One: The Payday Loan Prison

Lisa was broke. Needed $300 for rent. Took a payday loan. $45 fee. "Easy money," they said. But when payday came, she couldn't cover both the loan and her bills. She rolled it over. The $300 became $900 in debt within 6 months.

That lender didn't care if she ever escaped. They wanted her trapped. Her struggle was their business model.

The Economics of Suffering

Payday loans: $9 billion a year industry, built on poverty.

Pharmaceuticals: $500 billion in drug sales, many for preventable diseases.

Private prisons: Billions in profit per year. Stock prices rise when arrests rise.

Entertainment industry: Billions from streaming, sports, and celebrity worship to keep you distracted.

You think it's random. It's designed. Every system around you has one motto: "Bleed them, don't kill them. Sick bodies pay longer than dead ones."

Case Study: The Prison Pipeline

The U.S. has 5% of the world's population, but 25% of the world's prisoners.

Private prison companies like CoreCivic and GEO Group make billions annually.

They lobby for harsher laws because more inmates = more profit.

A young hustler thinks his arrest is bad luck. In reality, he's a business asset in chains.

Story Two: The Fast Food Funeral

Darnell ate fast food daily. Cheap, quick, addictive. At 52, he had diabetes. At 56, his leg was amputated. At 59, he was gone.

McDonald's stock soared while his health collapsed. His pain was their dividend.

Street vs. Corporate Profits

Street Hustle:

Hustler profits from someone's addiction.

Quick money, high risk, violent collapse.

Corporate Hustle:

Corporations profit from millions of addictions: sugar, nicotine, opioids, credit.

Slow money, low risk, generational wealth.

One is called criminal. The other is called capitalism. Same playbook. Different lawyers.

Numbers Don't Lie

Opioid epidemic: Purdue Pharma made billions pushing OxyContin, knowing it was addictive. Over 500,000 dead.

Food industry: 75% of grocery products have added sugar.

Medical bankruptcy: 66% of U.S. bankruptcies caused by medical bills.

Student loans: $1.7 trillion industry. Interest keeps students in lifelong debt.

The pain isn't accident. It's engineered profit.

Story Three: The Entertainment Escape

Tasha worked a dead-end job. Bills stacked. Stress heavy. But every night, she binged Netflix, watched celebrity gossip, scrolled TikTok.

Her escape became her sedation. Her pain kept her consuming. And while she laughed at reality shows, billion-dollar corporations laughed at her.

Case Study: Bread and Circuses

In ancient Rome, leaders gave the people "bread and circuses" — cheap food and endless entertainment — to keep them distracted while the empire collapsed.

Today, it's McDonald's and Netflix. Cheap food, endless shows. The same play, updated for Wi-Fi.

The Trap of Silent Bleeding

The genius of the shadow war is subtlety.

A gunshot is obvious.

A heart attack at 45 from stress is quiet.

A foreclosure from predatory loans is quiet.

A family split from financial strain is quiet.

They don’t need riots. They need routine. Quiet suffering that never makes headlines but keeps the machine fed.

Story Four: The Sick Worker

Andre had high blood pressure. His boss knew. His insurance company knew. His pharmacy knew. Everybody profited from his sickness. Pills monthly. Checkups quarterly. Insurance premiums yearly.

When he died at 50, his family cried. But the system smiled. Because even in death, his debt kept paying.

Numbers Don’t Lie (Again)

Obesity market: $315 billion annually in weight-loss products, gym memberships, diet pills. Many don’t work, but they keep you buying.

Credit card debt: Americans owe over $1 trillion. Banks profit billions in interest.

Funeral industry: $20 billion annually. Even your death is monetized.

From womb to tomb, your pain is priced.

Case Study: The Black Community

Hair relaxers & skin lighteners: Billion-dollar industries profiting off insecurity.

Liquor & tobacco stores: Flooded in poor neighborhoods.

Predatory landlords: Charging double rent for worse housing.

The pain of Black communities is not just tolerated. It's harvested.

The Warning, The Story, The Lesson

The Warning:

Your suffering is not random. It's a business. If you don't fight back, you'll die as someone else's profit margin.

The Story:

A man worked 40 years. Paid into insurance. Paid into loans. Paid into pills. When he died, his family discovered his estate was negative. He had given his entire life to the system — and left nothing but debt.

The Lesson:

The shadow war can't be won by denial. Only by awareness, discipline, and ownership. The more pain you privatize, the less they can monetize.

Closing Manifesto

This is the shadow war. Not fought with bullets. Fought with bills. Not fought with bloodshed. Fought with slow bleeding.

Your suffering is their salary. Your pain is their profit. Your silence is their weapon. But your awareness is their enemy. And once you see the war, you can't unsee it.

So fight back. Eat clean. Own your debt. Protect your body. Build your circle. Teach your children.

Because the only way to starve the machine is to stop feeding it your pain.

Bonus Chapter— Time: The Richest Currency

You Don't Spend Money — You Spend Time

"They told you to chase money. They never told you money is just a receipt for your time."

Every paycheck is proof you sold your hours. Every bill is proof you traded your life for survival. Money feels like the prize, but the real prize is time — and it's the only currency you never get back.

The rich know this. That's why they buy time with money. The poor don't. That's why they sell time for money.

Story One: The Father Who Missed His Kids

Marcus worked 60 hours a week. Always tired. Always grinding. One day his son asked, "Dad, why don't you ever come to my games?"

Marcus said, "I'm working to give you a better life."

But years later, his son didn't remember the money. He remembered the absence. The real price wasn't the bills Marcus paid. It was the time he could never buy back.

The Math of Time

24 hours a day.

8 hours for work.

2 hours commuting.

1 hour prepping.

7 hours sleeping.

6 hours left — and most of that eaten by chores, screens, and distractions.

By the time most people finish surviving, they have maybe 1 hour of true freedom per day. That's not life. That's prison with Wi-Fi.

Case Study: Millionaires Buy Time

Wealthy people hire cleaners, assistants, drivers.

They outsource what wastes time.

They use money to buy back hours so they can focus on wealth-building.

Meanwhile, workers use their time to chase money that never buys freedom. That's why the gap grows: one side compounds time, the other side wastes it.

Story Two: The Woman With No Weekends

Tasha worked retail. Every weekend. Every holiday. Ten years gone. She looked up and realized she missed weddings, birthdays, family reunions. She sold her prime years for $15 an hour.

The store made millions. She made memories of exhaustion. That's the theft of time.

Street vs. Corporate Time

Street Hustler:

Chases quick flips. Spends all night in chaos. Life expectancy shortened by stress and danger.

Corporate Worker:

Trades 40 years for retirement at 65. By then, body is tired, dreams are gone.

Both sell the richest currency cheap. Both die regretting lost time.

Numbers Don't Lie

Average worker spends 90,000 hours at work in a lifetime.

Commuting eats 10,000 hours.

Americans spend 7 years of life watching TV.

Average person spends 2.5 hours/day on social media = 7 years gone.

Add it up: half your life sold, scrolled, or stolen.

Story Three: The Man Who Retired Too Late

Anthony dreamed of traveling the world. Worked until 67. Retired. Two years later, diagnosed with cancer. Died at 70.

He traded 40 years of time for three years of freedom. The math didn't math.

Case Study: 80/20 Principle

Italian economist Vilfredo Pareto discovered the 80/20 rule: 80% of results come from 20% of actions. Wealthy people live by this. They cut wasted time, focus on the 20% that multiplies.

Poor people drown in the 80% — busy work, distractions, toxic relationships. That's why they stay broke.

The Trap of "Later"

The system teaches you to put life off.

"Work now, live later."

"Retire at 65."

"Enjoy yourself after the grind."

But later never comes. Later is stolen by sickness, stress, layoffs, death. The only time you own is now.

Story Four: The Builder Who Reclaimed Hours

Keon worked 9–5. Instead of wasting nights, he used 7–11 to build his side hustle. Four hours a night. Within 3 years, he escaped the job.

He didn't wait for later. He weaponized now.

Numbers Don't Lie (Again)

Bill Gates reads 50 books a year.

Warren Buffet spends 80% of his time reading.

Average worker spends 4 hours/day watching TV.

Same hours. Different usage. Same 24. Different futures.

Story Five: The Funeral Reflection

At funerals, nobody talks about money. They talk about time: the moments shared, the memories made. That's proof: time is the only currency that matters.

The Art of Time Mastery

Audit your hours. Track where they go.

Cut the leaks. Social media, gossip, TV.

Invest hours. Skills, building, health, family.

Buy back time. Use money to free hours.

Protect time. Guard it like treasure.

Case Study: Corporate Time Theft

Meetings with no purpose.

Emails that waste hours.

“Busy work” that builds nothing.

Corporations design time drains to keep workers docile. Because if you had real time, you’d build your exit.

The Warning, The Story, The Lesson

The Warning:

If you don’t master your time, someone else will. They’ll rent your hours cheap, and you’ll die realizing you gave away the richest currency.

The Story:

A man worked his whole life for “overtime pay.” Died at 60. His children got nothing but memories of absence. His money died with him. His time was gone forever.

The Lesson:

Money can be regained. Time cannot. Treat time like gold, or you'll die rich in regret.

Closing Manifesto

Time is the only true wealth. Money is paper. Cars rust. Chains tarnish. But time — once it's gone, it never returns.

Your time is your life. Your hours are your empire. Don't trade eternity for a paycheck. Don't trade decades for debt. Don't waste years scrolling screens. Guard your time. Multiply your time. Own your time.

Because when the clock stops, the receipts of money don't matter. Only the investment of time does. And the richest man alive is the one who died owning his hours.

Bonus Chapter — The Blueprint for Community: Beyond the Individual

One Free Man is Vulnerable. One Free Community is Untouchable.

"They told you to chase success alone. They never told you one man can be killed, but a community can't be erased."

Individual freedom is fragile. You can build wealth, health, and legacy — but if your children inherit a broken community, the system will swallow them back into poverty. That's why the blueprint must extend beyond the individual. Because one free man is a target. One free community is a nation.

Story One: The Lone Builder

Darius left the hood. Made six figures. Moved to the suburbs. Thought he was safe. But his kids grew up isolated, no culture, no foundation. They fell into drugs and identity loss.

His wealth bought escape but not protection. Because freedom alone is fragile.

The Math of Collective Power

One dollar alone feeds one family.

One dollar circulating in community feeds hundreds.

One man's knowledge dies with him.

One community's knowledge outlives generations.

That's the blueprint: circulation, multiplication, preservation.

Case Study: Tulsa's Black Wall Street

600 businesses.

15 doctors.

21 churches.

A hospital, schools, theaters, banks.

Money circulated 19 times before leaving. That's why Tulsa thrived. It wasn't just individual hustlers. It was collective commitment.

The bombs didn't just kill people. They killed the circulation. They killed the system. Because community is the real threat.

Story Two: The Block That Bought Back the Hood

A group of barbers, teachers, mechanics, and single mothers pooled money. Bought an abandoned strip mall. Opened a grocery store, a daycare, and a clinic. The city ignored them at first. But soon, the neighborhood had jobs, food, and safety.

They weren't rich. But they were free together.

Street vs. Corporate Community

Street:

Crews build loyalty but collapse because vision stops at survival.

No contracts, no structure. Jealousy and chaos eat them alive.

Corporate:

Boards, co-ops, trusts. Wealth passed quietly, legally, endlessly.

Circulation systems protect families for centuries.

Both are groups. Only one is structured. That's the difference between collapse and continuity.

Numbers Don't Lie

Immigrant groups: Dollar circulates 12–20 times before leaving.

Black communities: Dollar circulates 6 hours.

Co-ops: Produce $500 billion annually worldwide.

The system doesn't fear rich individuals. It fears organized communities. That's why destruction of Black Wall Streets happened coast to coast — Tulsa, Rosewood, Wilmington.

Story Three: The Community Bank

Miss Hattie started a susu — a rotating savings circle. Ten families put in $100/month. Every month, one family got $1,000.

Within two years, five families owned homes. The bank never touched a dime. That's collective blueprint.

Case Study: Collective Power vs. Individual Escape

1980s crack epidemic: Individuals escaped, moved away. Communities collapsed.

Jewish communities: Built schools, banks, hospitals for their own. Collective power preserved them.

The difference ain't luck. It's blueprint.

The Trap of Lone Wolves

The system celebrates the lone wolf — "self-made," "I did it myself." But that myth is poison. Because lone wolves die quick. Packs survive.

If you build alone, your wealth can be erased in one generation. If you build with community, your wealth becomes infrastructure.

Story Four: The Community That Refused Eviction

Developers tried to buy out a neighborhood. Residents banded together. Created a land trust. Refused to sell. Instead, they renovated, built gardens, created a community-owned grocery.

Developers lost. The people won.

That's blueprint.

Numbers Don't Lie (Again)

Life insurance pools: 100 families × $100/month = $120,000/year. Enough to cover funerals, emergencies, investments.

Community-owned land trusts: Hundreds exist today, preserving affordable housing.

Group economics: Marcus Garvey's UNIA had 4 million members worldwide pooling resources.

The math proves: community multiplies freedom.

The Community Blueprint

Land: Own soil, or you own nothing.

Food: Gardens, farms, co-ops. No food deserts.

Health: Clinics, holistic centers, fitness systems.

Education: Schools teaching truth, finance, survival.

Economy: Credit unions, susu systems, co-ops.

Security: Community patrols, legal defense funds.

Culture: Arts, music, spiritual systems that preserve identity.

That's not utopia. That's blueprint.

The Warning, The Story, The Lesson

The Warning:

If you build alone, the system will eat your children. If you build together, the system will fear you.

The Story:

A millionaire bought houses for his kids. But the neighborhood collapsed. Drugs, crime, poverty swallowed them. His money couldn't save them. Another man wasn't rich, but his community pooled, built schools, and land trusts. His children thrived.

The Lesson:

Individual success is fragile. Community success is forever. If you want freedom, build circles, not cages.

Closing Manifesto

One man free is survival. One family free is comfort. One community free is revolution.

Freedom that dies with you was never freedom. The only proof you lived free is a community that can't be enslaved again.

Buy the land. Start the susu. Open the school. Build the clinic. Protect the block.

Because the future ain't written by individuals. The future is written by communities who refused to die.

Closing Manifesto

The system wants you fragile. They want you scared of no. They want you silenced by rejection. Because fragile builders never build.

But hear this:

Every no is a seed. Every rejection is a brick. Every slammed door is proof you knocked. And if you keep knocking, the world has no choice but to open.

Don't fear no. Collect it. Wear it. Stack it like currency. Because rejection ain't failure. Rejection is flight fuel. And the ones who fly the highest are the ones who paid the most no's.

The Journey You Just Walked

If you've made it here, you already know this ain't no self-help fairy tale. This is not "10 tips to get rich quick." This is not a motivational speech to pump you up for two weeks before you collapse back into the same cycle.

This book was a war manual. A survival guide. A mirror.

We started where the system started with you — The Programming. The lies in school, church, jobs, telling you obedience was virtue. Then we exposed The Institutionalization, showing how work, prison, and even military all run the same cage. Then we showed you the math — The Math Ain't Mathin' — proving how no matter how hard you grind, the numbers were rigged.

But we didn't leave you in despair. We walked into action: The First Move, because motion beats fear. Becoming the Product, because you sell yourself before you sell anything. If I Quit, I Can Fly, because quitting chains is the first step of flight.

We fortified with discipline, because freedom without control collapses. We mastered money, because dollars are soldiers. We built legacy, because if it dies with you, it was never real. And then we defined Final Freedom, because survival isn't enough. You were born to outlive the system, not just escape it.

But that was only the beginning.

The Bonus Chapters sharpened the weapons. The Circle showed you that people are the price. Health taught you the temple must stand. The Hustler's MBA taught you business doesn't need permission. The Digital Trap exposed the new chains on your eyes. The Art of Rejection showed you no's are rent for flight. The Shadow War revealed how they profit off your pain. Time taught you the richest currency. And Community tied it all together, proving one man free is fragile, but a community free is unstoppable.

That is the blueprint. But blueprints mean nothing if you don't build.

Story One: The Builder vs. The Dreamer

Two men read the same book. Both were moved. Both saw the truth.

The first man closed it, nodded, said, “That was powerful,” and went back to scrolling, working, and waiting for permission. Ten years later, he was the same man, only older.

The second man closed it, stood up, and started building. He changed his circle. He changed his body. He flipped his money. He bought land. He taught his children. He linked arms with others and created a community. Ten years later, his life was unrecognizable.

Both men saw the same blueprint. Only one picked up the bricks.

The Three Wars

Freedom is not handed. It's fought. And the wars are clear:

The Inner War: Discipline, fear, rejection. Conquering your own weakness.

The Outer War: Money, systems, institutions. Flipping their weapons into yours.

The Eternal War: Legacy and community. Building structures that outlive bullets, bombs, and betrayals.

Lose the inner war, you never start. Lose the outer war, you never last. Lose the eternal war, you never matter.

Case Study: Generations as Proof

First generation fights to survive.

Second generation fights to stabilize.

Third generation fights to expand.

Fourth generation either rules or repeats the curse.

Your family is either compounding freedom or compounding slavery. Your bloodline is either multiplying or leaking.

The proof of your life ain't your car. Ain't your chain. Ain't your resume. The proof is whether your grandchildren will still be free.

Story Two: The Remembered vs. The Forgotten

In a graveyard, two headstones stand side by side.

One man worked, paid bills, obeyed, stayed quiet. His children forgot him within one generation.

The other man fought, built, sacrificed. He left land, stories, systems. His name is still spoken in his bloodline a hundred years later.

The difference wasn't talent. It was blueprint.

The Law of Multiplication

One disciplined man can build wealth.

One disciplined family can build legacy.

One disciplined community can build a nation.

But without structure, freedom evaporates. Without blueprint, bloodlines repeat cages.

This is why every empire that thrived had schools, land, laws, and culture. Not just money. Not just hype. Systems.

You are not just building for yourself. You are blueprinting for eternity.

Numbers Don't Lie

Black spending power: $1.6 trillion annually.

Black wealth gap: White families hold 8x more wealth.

Black dollar leaves community in 6 hours.

We have the soldiers (money). We lack the generals (discipline, systems, community).

If $1.6 trillion was circulated like Tulsa did in 1921, you'd see freedom in one generation. But without blueprint, it leaks into chains.

The Final Warning

If you don't act now, the cycle will repeat. Your children will inherit your cage. And your grandchildren won't even remember your name.

Freedom is not survival. Freedom is system. And systems don't build themselves.

The Final Lesson

Everything you read in this book boils down to this:

Your body is your first business. Guard it.

Your circle is your mirror. Sharpen it.

Your money is your army. Deploy it.

Your time is your gold. Protect it.

Your legacy is your proof. Build it.

Your community is your fortress. Defend it.

If you neglect any of these, your empire crumbles. If you build all of them, your name becomes immortal.

The Final Story: The Rememberer

There is an old figure in every tradition — the griot, the elder, the Rememberer. The one who carries the stories, who keeps the truth alive.

This book was written in that spirit. To remind you of what was stolen. To warn you of the traps. To hand you the weapons. To leave you with no excuse.

Because the Rememberer's job is not to entertain. It's to awaken.

Closing Manifesto

You have been programmed. Institutionalized. Trapped in broken math. Sedated with comfort. Bled in silence. Distracted by screens. Robbed of time. Poisoned in body. Stripped of community.

And yet — you are still here. Which means it is not too late.

Freedom is not given. It is built. Freedom is not survival. It is system. Freedom is not a dream. It is discipline, money, legacy, and community tied together. Freedom is not for later. Freedom is for now.

So rise. Quit what kills you. Build what outlives you. Protect your temple. Flip your circle. Flip your money. Guard your hours. Sharpen your children. Link your neighbors. Plant seeds that bombs cannot burn.

Because the day you die, the system will cheer if your name dies with you. But if your legacy, your family, your community lives on — then you won the war.

Final freedom is not about you. It's about eternity.

And the blueprint is in your hands.

Now build.

About the Author

Patrice Shabazz is a son of North Carolina — raised by hardship, hardened by experience, and healed through truth. A sharp voice forged in poverty, he writes to expose the systems that keep everyday people buried under debt, silence, and struggle. His words don't just teach — they testify.

Patrice's mission reaches beyond the page. He is actively working to build a self-sustainable community rooted in group economics, accountability, and liberation. Through books, outreach, and strategic action, he's not just telling stories — he's blueprinting solutions.

If you are a like-minded individual, a builder, a visionary, or simply someone curious about how we rise together, reach out: patriceshabazz39@gmail.com

---

"A lone runner may reach the hill first — but a village crosses mountains."

— Patrice Shabazz

Led by Patrice Shabazz | Founder, Exclusive Heights

We're building more than a neighborhood — we're building a future.

The Vision

Imagine 300–500 acres of land, powered by solar, growing our own food, raising livestock, creating jobs, and raising children in a safe, educated, self-governed environment.

This isn't a dream. This is a blueprint.

We're forming a 1,000-person self-sustainable Black-led community rooted in:

- Group economics
- Cooperative living
- Clean food, clean water, clean energy
- Vocational training & land-based education
- Mental, physical, and financial healing

The Math & Mission

- Goal: $12,000 per person x 1,000 = $12 million
- Covers: Land (300–500 acres), infrastructure, housing, farming, solar, schools, tradespaces, and startup capital for community-owned businesses.

Every dollar goes into ownership, food security, and generational wealth — not rent.

Who We're Looking For

We're recruiting:

- Skilled tradespeople: Electricians, Plumbers, Builders, Farmers, HVAC, Welders
- Educators & Mentors: Teachers, Counselors, Homeschoolers, Youth Leaders
- Medical & Holistic Health: Nurses, CNAs, Herbalists, Wellness Coaches
- Tech & Media: Web Designers, Editors, Content Creators
- General Builders: Visionaries willing to work, grow, and invest in change

---

Why Join?

- Be part of a legacy project
- Live and work with purpose
- Help build Black independence
- Escape survival mode and enter sustainability
- Your name will be on the foundation of a new nation within a nation

---

Support & Donate

Help fund the first phase:

- [GoFundMe gofund.me/637427e2]
- Cash App: $ExclusiveHeights

Every donation brings us one step closer to land, infrastructure, and freedom.

Get Involved

Contact: patriceshabazz39@gmail.com
Based in North Carolina — open to national collaboration

———

"A system built to bury us… won't survive the ones who plant back."
— Patrice Shabazz

Made in the USA
Monee, IL
05 November 2026

67386757R00152